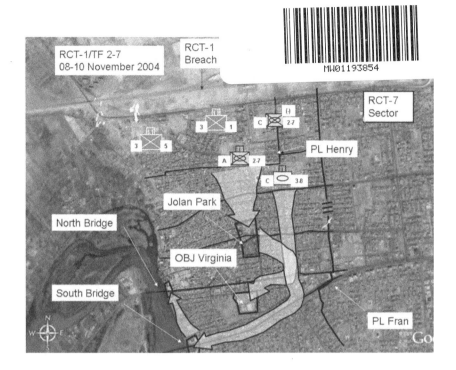

Second Battle of Fallujah: Phase I map

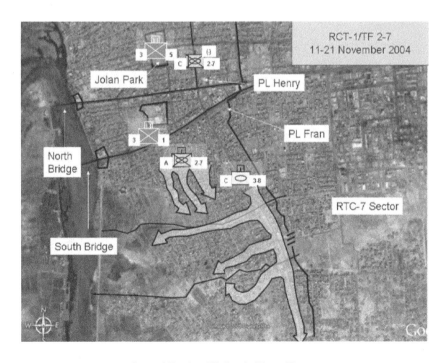

Second Battle of Fallujah: Phase II map

GHOSTS

OF

FALLUJAH

For Robert —
Hate war, love the
American Soldier!

Coly O'Hl
11/20/18

GHOSTS

OF

FALLUJAH

COLEY D. TYLER

Deeds Publishing | Atlanta

Published by Deeds Publishing in Athens, GA
www.deedspublishing.com

Printed in The United States of America

978-1-947309-04-3

Books are available in quantity for promotional or premium use. For information, email info@deedspublishing.com.

First Edition, 2018

10 9 8 7 6 5 4 3 2 1

DEDICATION

To members of the Second Battalion, Seventh Cavalry of Operation
Iraqi Freedom II, and past Seventh Cavalry Troopers.

and

To my closest Family Veterans, retired Colonel Herbert Daniel Tyler
Sr., Herbert Daniel Tyler Jr., and Arnold Irvin Dixon Jr.

also

To members of the First Cavalry Division, First Marine Division,
graduates of the United States Military Academy, US Military
Veterans, US Military Families, and future leaders wherever they may
be found.

ACKNOWLEDGEMENTS

I wrestled with the idea of writing a book for many years, but being uncomfortable about exposing my innermost thoughts to the world prevented me from doing anything about it until I was stationed at West Point from 2009—2012. My reservations remain, but at this point in my life, I am willing to take a chance and I believe more good will come from this project than naught. Who knows, maybe someone else out there may be positively impacted by this story. While this is a personal account of my involvement with the 2nd Battalion, 7th Cavalry (2-7 CAV), I do my best to tell my story with consideration for the bigger picture of the unit history, the great soldiers that have made it up—past and present, lessons in leadership, and the "so what" factor that makes this applicable to life in general. I am very proud of being a member of 2-7 CAV, "Ghost" as we were called back then, and deeply desire to share our portion of its storied history. I am certain it deserves to be heard.

There are several people that merit special recognition for their advice, assistance, material support, and belief that I could accomplish this momentous task. Dr. Ralph Pim, retired Colonel (Col.) "Stretch" Dunn, Col. Lee Gentile Jr., author Mr. Jim Lawrence, editor-journalist Mr. Matt McAllester, author Mr. Matt Matthews, and author Mr. McKendree Long all helped get this book off the ground. These men spent hours reading, reviewing, commenting on, suggesting improvements, and providing input to the manuscript. It would not have been possible without them. Former Ghosts Mike Erwin and Eric Hough provided a large majority of the pictures you see throughout which really brings the story to life through their photographs.

I would be remiss if I did not thank my family for putting up with me while I threw myself into this project also, trying to complete a first draft just a few months before a move to Korea and then the years hence that I have continued to inch closer to the ultimate goal of publication. Erin Charlene "Charley", my wife, has put up with a lot from me since we were married in 2003, least of which was the writing of this book. Actually, the book process helped improve our relationship by forcing me to deal with one of my more difficult character traits she has had to put up with, which is my poor ability to share my feelings, especially when it comes to Iraq. Working together on getting this book published offered her an opportunity to experience this time in my life and give her a better understanding of how it has molded and shaped me into the man I am today.

As for my children: Caden Daniel, Campbell Charlene, Cooper Dixon, and Colby Jane this is a small, but important part of my legacy to them. Other than just being daddy, at some point I want them to know who I was, particularly when it comes to my service to the Nation. I hope this book puts into context all the lessons I shared with them growing up, it will aid them in their character development, and its words will be a helpful guide on their life's journey.

Although I based this book on historical facts, a lot of which I share with the reader, this is still a personal narrative. The primary sources are my own recollections and the detailed interviews conducted by Mr. Matt Matthews with so many 2-7 CAV veterans after the battle. All thoughts, feelings, opinions, and characterizations; however, are mine alone. I do not attempt or claim to speak for the United States (US) Government, the US Army, or any other persons affiliated with the events of this book. In an effort to reveal the human element of service in a time of war, I mention many individuals I interacted with on a regular basis. I know there are hundreds of others that deserve inclusion and thanks for their contributions that you will not read about by name in this book; however, the people you do read about are symbolic of all members of 2-7 CAV from bottom to top. So, if you ever meet a Ghost of 2-7 CAV from Operation Iraqi Freedom II (OIF II), tell them thank you for a job well done.

I begin each segment and/or chapter of this story with an excerpt from the book *Gates of Fire* by Steven Pressfield. His book tells the tale of some of the most renowned warriors in all of history, the Spartans, fighting at the Battle of Thermopylae. Mr. Pressfield does an extraordinary job at putting some of the feelings, virtues, and beliefs of professional soldiers, from ancient Greece to the present, into words that surely sets the stage for each part of this book. When I reported to 2-7 CAV for the first time in Iraq back in 2004, reading his book was one of the first tasks I was given by my battalion commander. I felt his expectations of me, our unit, how we would fight, and the seriousness of our business were very clear when he required me to read that book.

Gates of Fire is highly recommended professional reading by many military leaders, including the late retired Lieutenant General (Lt. Gen.) Harold G. Moore. For those imbued with the warrior spirit, it has a very powerful and gripping influence; an influence I still feel very strongly today. It was foundational to the development of my company command (tour number two in Iraq) philosophy and military ethos I worked to instill in my Soldiers, some of which I will share in later chapters. For now, I will just tell you we were the Spartans and our motto was: "Warriors First!" Throughout the text, I try to minimize the use of too many military acronyms (for those non-military readers), but do include a glossary at the the back of the book.

Ghosts of Fallujah is a humble attempt at chronicling a very meaningful and historic period in my life and for one of the most famous military units in American history, underscored by the invaluable leadership lessons garnered along the way. These lessons come from Lt. Gen. Moore, other 7th Cavalry leaders, and ones of my own I discovered during this personal journey. I hope as you read this book you find something that in some small way might benefit you in your life. In the words of Lt. Gen. Moore, "One's story is a powerful learning tool for others—no matter the story. There is so much to learn from others in this way...Based upon this I am willing to share my story, if it is of interest to others. If not, just skip the boring stuff."[1]

—*Coley D. Tyler*

---

1 Lt. Gen. Hal Moore, "No Holds Barred: A Leadership Conversation with LTG Hal Moore," DRAFT (2009), http://www.auburnschools.org/ahs/llalexander/HMLA/No%20Holds%20Barred%20Hal%20Moore%20Conversation%20July%2029%202009.doc.

CONTENTS

PART I

PROLOGUE

PROLOGUE

APRIL 29, 1997

War, and preparation for war, call forth all that is noble and hon-
orable in a man. It unites him with his brothers and binds them
in selfless love, eradicating in the crucible of necessity all which is
base and ignoble.[2]   —Steven Pressfield, *Gates of Fire*

In the very beginning, this story [*Ghosts of Fallujah*] and how I ended
up in Fallujah in the first place began with a made-for-television movie.
That movie was *North and South.* That's right, the television adaptation of
the 1980's based upon the John Jakes novels: *North and South, Love and
War,* and *Heaven and Hell,* starring famous actors and actresses such as
Patrick Swayze, James Read, Leslie-Anne Down and Kirstie Alley, just
to name a few. *North and South,* the TV mini-series, captured my imagi-
nation like nothing else as a kid growing up in the remote mountains of
Western North Carolina. Nothing else had a bigger impact on setting
the course of my future life. *North and South* was my first exposure to the
United States Military Academy (USMA) at West Point, New York, and
the military profession. Albeit quite theatrical and melodramatic, this
story captivated me beyond explanation. I knew from the moment I first
saw that film that I wanted to go to West Point and be an Army officer.
    My parents recorded *North and South Book I* and *Book II* on several

---

2 Steven Pressfield, Gates of Fire: An Epic Novel of the Battle of Thermopylae (New
York, NY: Bantam Dell, 1998), 137.

3

VHS (Video Home System) tapes when they first aired. I watched them religiously from about 5th grade on, Mrs. Fouts' fifth grade class to be exact, at Cowee Elementary School, a "Gem-dandy Place to Learn." I watched them in the summer time mostly so I would not drive everyone crazy with my recitations, except my sister. If I was not watching and reciting it, I was out in the woods behind my house reenacting it. I would imagine myself gloriously serving my country at places like Churubusco (Mexican War), Bull Run or any other battle of the Civil War. Even though that was many decades ago, I can still recount almost every line from the eighteen-hour long movie.

Attending West Point became the ultimate ambition of my young life because of that movie. My grandmother, affectionately known by all as Miss Jane, helped fuel the fire with the gift of a book about West Point and telling me about my great-great uncle. As the matriarch of our family, she knew our family history going back to the 1600s and was always eager to share with her inquisitive grandson. My great-great uncle's name was William E. Coffin Jr., USMA Class of 1916, who was also an Army football player (letterman in 1914/15) and served in World War I as a Major (Maj.) in the 59th Infantry, 4th Division, American Expeditionary Forces. His letterman plaque still hangs in the stairwell of the north entrance of Hayes Gymnasium in Arvin Cadet Physical Development Center on the grounds of USMA at West Point. She also reminded me that my grandfather (Herbert Daniel Tyler Sr.), my dad (Herbert Daniel Tyler Jr.), and my uncle (Arnold Irvin Dixon Jr.) had all served also as it was not a fact they flaunted about because of their deep-rooted humility.

From that moment on, in my mind there was not going to be anything or anyone to keep me from being Orry Main or George Hazard (central characters from *North and South*) as I went to West Point and then served in the US Army. I think this yearning at such an early age caused my parents quite a bit of worry because they knew I had set the bar high and I still had a long way to go before I could apply (I was only

10). They knew that a lot could happen before then and that my poor eyesight might be a factor out of my control that could very well keep me from admission. I stuck to my plan, never lost my desire, got a waiver for my eyesight, and in December 1995, received a letter stating I had been accepted to West Point's Class of 2000. By chance, hard work, divine intervention, or maybe fate, my dream had come true.

My time at West Point afforded me the opportunity to begin a journey that culminated with the book you are reading now and became one of the most defining times in my life, definitely in my military career. That journey began 29 April 1997 when I stood in line as a lowly Plebe (USMA freshman) at the Cadet Bookstore on the 4th Floor of Thayer Hall with my copy of *We Were Soldiers Once…and Young* written by Lt. Gen. Moore, who was one of America's greatest warriors and heroes, and Mr. Joe Galloway. I was there with one purpose and that was to see and meet the man that I had chosen to be my professional role model. I was there to see Lt. Gen. Moore and I would have waited in that line until hell froze over if required. I thought this was a once in a lifetime opportunity and I was not going to let it slip away.

As I stood in line, my life at the Academy passed through my mind and I knew it was about to be all-worthwhile. My life as a Plebe had been a living hell since I had reported for "Beast Barracks" (Cadet Basic Training) ten months earlier. I was at the very bottom of the totem pole for the first time in my life and I was having trouble dealing with Plebe life. My resolve to prove to my family, myself, and the rest of the world that I had not made a mistake had been put to the test. Fear of failure and my strong desire to achieve the goals I had set for myself compelled me to stay the course and hold my own at the Academy.

It did not hurt to have a core group of friends to lean on. I made some of the best and longest lasting friends of my life during my time at the Academy, just like Orry and George. One was an Army brat named Matt and the other Micah, from North Dakota. The fact that I had made it past Recognition (period in the school year where Plebes are finally afforded some basic privileges) helped a lot also. Along the way though I had a few upper-class cadets I equated to my own personal Elkanah Bents (the sworn enemy of Orry and George), which always seemed to make things worse. But, like them, I survived.

So, there I was standing in line at the Cadet Bookstore, thinking this moment was possible because I was persevering through the trials and tribulations of my Plebe year and that if I stayed committed, my future might possibly offer me a career as great as the man who sat just a few feet from me. I knew back then as a Soldier, I wanted to be like Lt. Gen. Moore. I just hoped I could live up to his example—emulate, lead, and serve like him. At that moment, the future held so many possibilities and I felt on top of the world, even from my bottom dwelling plebian status!

That brief meeting and few moments of polite conversation was enough to reassure me that I had chosen wisely in my professional role model. From that day forward, I tried my best to follow in Lt. Gen. Moore's footsteps. My cadet career was nowhere near stellar, even though I tried very hard and did my best. I managed to graduate right smack dab in the middle of the class, which was only slightly higher than Lt. Gen. Moore's class rank. I selected Fort Hood, Texas, home of the 1st Cavalry Division (1CD), as my first duty station. I chose to become a Field Artilleryman (Infantry a close second, but could not resist the firepower of the "King of Battle") when the time came to choose my branch during my Firstie (USMA Senior) year. I volunteered for and graduated from the US Army Airborne and Ranger courses. My officership began with an assignment to the 3rd Brigade (BDE), 1CD "Greywolf", a unit Lt. Gen. Moore was a member of and commanded in Vietnam, upon my arrival in Texas. Little did I know at the time though, but I would have even more opportunities to serve in the shadow of Lt. Gen. Moore in my career.

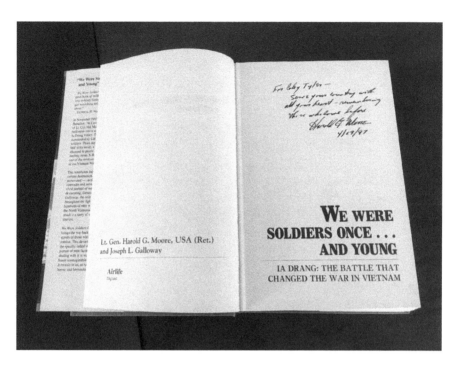

My signed copy of *We Were Soldiers Once…and Young* (4/29/97)
Source: Photo courtesy of Coley Tyler

PART II

AN UNFORESEEN JOURNEY

1. CITY OF MOSQUES

If you show fear, they will be afraid. If you project courage, they will match it in kind. Our deportment here must not differ from any other campaign. On the one hand, no extraordinary precautions; on the other, no unwonted recklessness. Above all, the little things. Maintain your men's training schedule without alteration. Omit no sacrifice to the gods. Continue your gymnastics and drill-at-arms. Take time to dress your hair, as always. If anything, take more time.[3]   —Steven Pressfield, *Gates of Fire*

Fallujah—what a great place, said no one ever. Even coming into the Iraq War going on its second year (March 2004), I knew the reputation of the city that sat just west of Baghdad on the east bank of the Euphrates River. It was not friendly to Americans, and it was not friendly to the Interim Iraqi Government (IIG). In fact, I did not recall anyone, other than native Fallujans, that the inhabitants were friendly toward. Oft described as having "mean streets" or being the "most dangerous city in Iraq" was not lost on the astute scholar of war. Fallujah's geographic location (along the ancient path of the Silk Road) made it a critical crossroads of trade and commerce, both legal and illegal—"a way station for merchants, smugglers, and thieves crossing the desert."[4] Fallujah had

---

3 Ibid., 225.
4 Richard D. Camp, Operation Phantom Fury: The Assault and Capture of Fallujah, Iraq (Minneapolis, MN: Zenith Press, 2009), 11.

a centuries old history and tradition of highway robbery and lawlessness, leading most people to stop only as long as they had to for conducting business.[5] Mr. Paul Bremer, Administrator of the Coalition Provisional Authority of Iraq, commented on Fallujah's infamy in his memoir.

> *Fallujah had a well-earned reputation* as a tough town. A city of 300,000, Fallujah sprawled across a bend in the Euphrates, the crossroads of several traditional caravan trails west through the desert to Syria, which became useful smugglers' routes after the Gulf War when Saddam bypassed UN [United Nations] sanctions. When the British had taken over Mesopotamia from the Ottomans after World War I, the city was the center of a bloody rebellion.[6]

Despite its rough nature and reputation, Fallujah's placement on the map made it a monetarily prosperous city to control. Great nations and empires battled and contested for its rule since antiquity-18th century B.C. and the expansion of the Babylonian empire.[7] In the 1st century A.D. it was the Romans, Trojans, Arabs, and Persians fighting for control.[8] The Mongols sacked the town in 1258 A.D., left it in ruins until the Ottomans revived it in the 16th century, who then in turn defended it from the Persians (again) and finally Britain during the First World War.[9]

You can imagine the violent history of Fallujah had an impact on its residents. One of the city's defining characteristics by the early 2000's

---

5 Ibid.

6 Ahmed Mansur, Inside Fallujah: The Unembedded Story (Northampton, MA: Olive Branch Press, 2009), 21.

7 Richard S. Lowry, New Dawn: The Battles for Fallujah (New York, NY: Savas Beatie LLC, 2010), 4.

8 Ibid., 4-5.

9 Ibid., 5.

was "its historically strong resistance to invasion."[10] Not only was it re-
sistant to outsiders, it was strong in its religious devotion, leading to the
city being called by Iraqis as the "City of Mosques and Minarets."[11] It
was shortened to just the "City of Mosques" by American forces. The
religious devotedness of the city; however, did not keep those in Fallujah
from committing some brutal and horrific acts of violence well beyond
the call of "patriotic resistance." Mr. Bremer recounted,

> *The Fallujah crisis broke into* the open on the morning of Wednes-
> day, March 31 [2004]. A small convoy of SUVs carrying Black-
> water USA security guards was ambushed in the center of Fallu-
> jah. The gunmen raked the Americans' car with AK-47s [Russian
> automatic rifle]. Then the vehicle was set alight. Dancing in a
> frenzy, a mob of townsmen dragged the smoldering corpses from
> the wreckage and ripped at the charred flesh with shovels. Then
> two blackened, dismembered bodies were strung from the girders
> of the city's main bridge across the river.[12]

By the early fall of 2004, Fallujah was once again the center of American and Iraqi attention. Muqtada al-Sadr had briefly taken the spotlight
off the city during the summer with heavy fighting in Najaf featuring
none other than 2-7 CAV, which allowed the barbaric insurgents of Fallujah time to regroup after the April Operation Vigilant Resolve—First
Battle of Fallujah (the Marines' first attempt at pacifiing the unruly city
immediately following the Blackwater incident mentioned above by Mr.
Bremer). "Marines closed in after the burned bodies of four contractors
were mutilated and hung over a bridge in March," and at least 44 US
troops [had] been killed since fighting began in April with some 600

---

10 Mansur, 19.
11 Ibid.
12 Ibid., 26.

Iraqis reported killed and 1,200 injured reported *Newsday* correspondent Matt McAllester.[13]

It had become clear the country of Iraq could not move forward with such a blatant symbol of rebellion and the insurgent bastion it had become sitting in the backyard of the national capital. The IIG knew that to have successful elections in January 2005 something had to be done with the ever growing enemy forces in Fallujah. Mr. McAllester relayed the Iraqi government's sentiments on Fallujah in an 8 Novmber 2004 piece for *Newsday*.

> *Interim Prime Minister Ayad Allawi* said yesterday, shortly before the attack started, that action could be near. "We can't wait indefinitely," he said. "We have made our case very clear, that we have nothing with the people of Fallujah. On the contrary, the people of Fallujah have been asking us to really intervene as fast as we can and to salvage the people. They have been taken hostage by a bunch of terrorists and bandits and insurgents who were part of the old regime.[14]

Mr. McAllester also reported that, "US officials contend the city harbors a network of Baathist regime supporters, foreign malcontents and terrorists, including Abu Musab al- Zarqawi, whose group has admitted to the beheading of hostages. Another concern is that insurgents would disrupt Iraq's January elections."[15] Regardless if Fallujans were held hostage or complicit in these heinous acts, something had to be done about the ever-worsening situation in Fallujah.

The look of Fallujah matched the resident's mood, feelings, and demeanor. It did not look like a happy place. It was an ominous and men-

---

13 Matthew McAllester, "Long-planned attack begins," Newsday, November 8, 2004, A04.
14 Ibid.
15 Ibid.

acing-looking city. It was roughly four kilometers wide and three kilometers deep with the Euphrates on the western edge and nothing but
desert to the north, east, and south.[16] The periodic flooding of the river
and the massive quantities of rotting trash made the whole place stink
with putrid and nauseating smells. The highest structures of the city were
the minarets. All the other buildings were drab shades of gray, brown,
and sandstone.

A look out over the City of Mosques in all its splendor
Source: Photo courtesy of Mike Erwin

The city contained more than fifty thousand densely packed buildings in two thousand city blocks so close together that in places there
was only a couple of feet between them.[17] The streets were narrow as
well, except for a few wide boulevards and walls six to eight feet tall

---

16 Camp, 13.
17 Ibid.

surrounded every home, making each one its own miniature fortress. Ridding this town of the enemy was not going to be an easy task. The stage was set as "more than 10,000 US and Iraq troops [were] poised to battle some 3,000 insurgents believed to be holed up inside Fallujah."[18]

As I stood above the command post observing the opening salvos of the fight for Fallujah unfold, there were so many thoughts running through my mind. The history of this place was part of it. The history to be made was another. Major General (Maj. Gen.) Natonski had recently visited our headquarters and motivated us as only he could.

> *"The finest fighting force on* the face of the earth is right here," Marine Maj. Gen. Rich Natonski, commander of the ground forces in the attack, told the 2nd Battalion in a visit shortly before the assault began. "This is a hell of a team. Iraqi forces are fired up. We're going to kick some butt."[19]

This battle was going to be a huge deal. I was extremely excited to be a part of something so monumental. The sky was on fire with explosions of all types—artillery, airdropped bombs, AC-130 (airplane gunship)/helicopter cannon fire. The darkness was lit up bright as day with preparatory fires, all in support of our impending attack. I felt the rumble of the explosions deep in my chest. As a Soldier, I had finally arrived on the big stage. It was a cool evening with a little rain, the city stunk, and I was wet, dirty, and stinking already, but this was combat, as I had always envisioned it—dangerous, in austere conditions without all the amenities, battling for the greater good of a nation against a deplorable and inhumane enemy. Matt McAllester also witnessed the start of the battle writing,

> *The primary aim of the* full-scale pounding of the front line of homes is to kill the triggermen of the remote-control bombs that

---

18 McAllester, A04.
19 "Driving toward the heart of enemy," *Newsday*, November 9, 2004, A07.

are likely to prove the biggest threat to American and Iraqi army forces pushing into the city…. "We're going to rain holy terror down on this front row of buildings," Karcher said. "You should see a burning part of the city. They're all sandbagged and all fortified buildings."…"I feel for anybody who's bought real estate here in the past year," said [Command] Sgt. Maj. Timothy Mace…[20]

At the same time that I was excited for the role I would play in this historic battle, I knew it would not be all brass bands and glory. I felt conflicted as only a Soldier can about being excited to do one's duty, knowing that meant some would make the ultimate sacrifice. Lieutenant Colonel (Lt. Col.) Jim Rainey of course understood this.

"We're going to take some casualties," Lt. Col. Jim Rainey, 39, said, sitting in his Tactical Operations Center, a room created under canvas between military vehicles that has been his headquarters for several days. Early this morning, he moved it up to within a mile of the outskirts of Fallujah. "It's hard," he said. "I'm in charge of X number of guys and some of them are going to get hurt."[21]

He reminded us of the gravity of the situation in a briefing shortly before the fighting began when he left us with a final thought, "Don't leave your honor, values, or buddies on the battlefield."[22] The Second Battle of Fallujah was wrought with risk. Risk to our battalion, risk to our Marine brothers, and risk to the mission in Iraq. We had to succeed and do our jobs in a fashion that would withstand world scrutiny, and believe me; the City of Mosques provided plenty of risk in the court of public opinion.

---

20 Ibid.
21 "Long-planned attack begins," A04.
22 Ibid.

Another risky part of the American tactics…is the military's willingness to fire on mosques if insurgents fire from them first. No matter the justification of such tactics under international law, images or reports of U.S. soldiers firing on mosques does not play well in Iraq, the Muslim world at large, or in many non-Muslim countries around the world, where anti-war feeling is high. That's a price the commanders are prepared to pay if it means allowing their soldiers to defend themselves fully. At one stage on Friday morning, insurgents fired at Apache 14 [Bradley Fighting Vehicle number, not the helicopter] from a mosque. Under the military's rules of engagement, American soldiers are permitted to fire on any of Fallujah's 77 mosques if insurgents shoot from them first. "They brought this — to themselves," Rainey said in the afternoon, visibly upset by casualties his battalion had just sustained. "Every mosque we found weapons inside. They're the ones who don't respect Islam, not us." Apache 14's gunner shot through every window he could see. He pounded parts of the minaret, splinters of stone flying into the air. Abdelwahab grabbed the radio handset and listened in to what the commanders were discussing. An insurgent "hit a tank and the tank shot a main gun round through the mosque," reported Abdelwahab, whose father is Lebanese by birth and a Muslim. "Yeah, we gotta back off at least 300 meters. The Marines are going to drop a 300 pounder on the mosque."…Watson backed the Bradley away from the mosque, but the bomb never came. Officers later said they felt there were too many American vehicles in the vicinity to bomb the mosque without risk of a friendly fire incident. The morning wore on amid an ever-intensifying hail of mortars, RPG [Rocket Propelled Grenade] attacks, and small-arms fire. It was time for the two-pronged push to the south that Rainey, Twaddell, and the other senior officers had planned. The troops, after experiencing the early attack on Apache 14, might have assumed the worst was over for the day. It wasn't.[23]

As our battalion inched ever closer to the breach into the city and I was heading back to my post because my watch told me it was time to take my place, I thought to myself, "How did I end up here?" The crackling voice traffic on the radios quickly reminded me there were more pressing matters now and those types of questions would have to wait for another time and place.

---

23 "Guerilla's Paradise," *Newsday*, November 14, 2004, A03.

2. SENIOR NIGHT

As he had done at every engagement at which it had been my privilege to observe him, the king stripped and worked along-side his warriors, shirking nothing, but pausing to address individuals, calling by name those he knew, committing to memory the names and even nicknames of others heretofore unknown to him, often clapping these new mates upon the back in the manner of a comrade and friend. It was astonishing with what celerity these intimate words, spoken only to one man or two, were relayed warrior-to-warrior down the line, filling the hearts of all with courage.[24]   — Steven Pressfield, *Gates of Fire*

That other time and place turned out to be only a few short months after my return from OIF II. I knew the opportunity to make sense of my experience in Fallujah would be another time, I just did not expect it to be so soon after I returned from Iraq, regardless of whether I was aware of the process taking place or not. Although I started acknowledging changes in my feelings and perspective shortly after my return, it took many more years to realize a book might be the best mechanism to share all my thoughts. When I finally did so, I was astonished to realize I had been putting this book together in my subconscious. It started where so many other parts of our adult lives begin…high school.

---

24 Pressfield, 219-20.

There is no way, even in my wildest dreams, that I ever imagined I would be a guest speaker for a high school graduation class, much less my own high school alma mater. Nevertheless, there I was seated in the same old gym, the "Panther Den," on the campus of Franklin High School (FHS) in May of 2005, in my Class A's (Army dress uniform) nervous as hell about what was about to take place. My old guidance counselor, Mr. Tinsley, contacted my daddy when he found out I was back from Iraq to see if I would be willing to address the FHS Class of 2005. I immediately accepted and then was scared out of my mind when I realized I had no idea what to say. To say I second-guessed my decision is an understatement.

The occasion was Senior Night when the high school recognized all the accomplishments of the graduating class a few days prior to the graduation ceremony. The set up was the same as it had been when I attended my own Senior Night so many years ago. The gym was still stifling hot and humid, jam-packed with family and friends, and full of seniors with a gleam in their eye that said the whole world was at their fingertips. I continued to wonder what could I possibly share with the class that would mean something to them or that they would even listen to for that matter. Why did Mr. Tinsley even invite me? What made me qualified to speak to these kids and their parents? What had I accomplished or done that gave me license to address all these people?

It felt like so little had changed, while at the same time things were so different. All my old teachers were the same, the campus looked the same, the gym had not changed either; I could find my way around the campus blindfolded I had spent so much time there. I guess the only thing that had really changed was me.

With that realization in mind, I decided that should be what I spoke about. How had I changed from when I sat in those same chairs lined up neatly on the gray tarp laid out to protect the highly varnished and well-kept gym floor. How my thoughts from that time had evolved to how I felt now. I spent hours upon hours perfecting my address, wanting it to be just right. I knew many of the people there and I was deathly afraid that somehow, someway I was going to make a fool of myself. I remembered vividly the last public address I made at FHS; it was a part of a graded assignment in Mrs. Eldridge's 11th grade English class… and it was not pretty!

The assignment involved writing a speech, about what I cannot rightly recall, as the event was so traumatic that I have just plain forgotten. It came my turn to address the class, and as a timid, very shy and late-blooming high school boy there was nothing I feared more than having to do this. Not only that, the two young ladies that intrigued me most during my four years in high school were both in that class. It could not get any worse, or could it?

I got up from my chair with sweaty palms, shaky hands, and trembling body and took my place behind the podium. As I put my note cards down on the stand, I knocked them off all over the floor. I uttered under my breath (I thought), "Oh Lord," which got a chuckle from my classmates and then proceeded to knock my head on the corner of the lectern as I bent down to pick them up. The class was in an uproar and even my teacher was finding it hard to keep a straight face.

This was so funny to everyone that a reenactment of this event took place at my own Senior Night when our salutatorian and one of my best friends, Eric Kuker, gave his remarks. The students and he got a huge laugh out of it (in a friendly way honoring my clumsiness), and all the teachers not privy to the inside joke were shuffling around trying to help him out. It was quite comical. Therefore, as you can imagine, these recollections were ever in the forefront of my mind, as I was getting ready to address the graduating class. Good thing Charley was with me the whole way, too. I needed all the moral support I could get and she was seated right next to me the whole time. I am not sure how it would have turned out if she had not been there.

I am much more comfortable speaking on a more personal level, in small groups or to a few individuals. Even in command, I preferred to speak to my Soldiers at the smallest level possible. After the ceremony, I got the chance for more conversations like that and was back in my comfort zone, but to get to the post-address small group question and answer session, I had to face this crowd of around 1,500 people first. In my mind, I was thinking I would rather be on patrol in Iraq than face this, but I did it.

I spoke about three things that night, things I learned about life since high school and things the military taught me or caused me to realize. I didn't want to just share leadership lessons though, but something more equivalent to life lessons; lessons that I did not understand when I was eighteen seated at my own Senior Night, but wish I had heard. I wanted to express an understanding and perspective on life that only the ordeal of combat was truly able to help me comprehend. Simply put for now, these ideas were 1) God gave you life to enjoy all things, not just what you think you want; 2) life is short, take nothing for granted; 3) your legacy is relationships, nothing else. These three thoughts have become some of the basic principles that guide my life. The following chapters will reveal the evolution of this life philosophy of mine and other important leadership qualities that I discovered and experienced on my journey with the 7th Cavalry, heavily influenced by Lt. Gen. Moore's example. In order to do this, you must also have an understanding of the history and significance of the 7th Cavalry Regiment.

3. GARRYOWEN!

"You have never tasted freedom, friend," Dienekes spoke, "or you would know it is purchased not with gold, but steel."[25]

— Steven Pressfield, *Gates of Fire*

Now that you know some of the personal background of this story I want to share with you some of the history of the US 7th Cavalry Regiment to better put this journey into perspective. I have been a history person my whole life and it is fitting I ended up choosing a profession that holds the history and lineage of its past in such high regard. So high, in fact, it is hard to adequately describe or illustrate the pressure and expectations that history brings with it for a professional Soldier. Lt. Gen. Moore felt, "To know your past and to celebrate it in smart ways [parades, ceremonies, traditions, and heritage] is key to building the future and teamwork. There is little greater than carrying on the greatness of past tradition."[26] It is an actual feeling; however, sometimes a burdensome pressure, sometimes a positive motivation, but a tangible feeling nonetheless.

West Pointers sing a song that describes this sensation called "The Corps." This ballad, one of the first traditions instilled at the Academy, which you memorize and internalize from the first week of Beast Barracks does a brilliant job of expressing this supernatural phenomenon. The song acknowledges the contributions of the Long Gray Line (term

---

25 Ibid., 51.
26 Moore, 23.

for all the past graduates of the Academy who wore the famous cadet gray uniforms), the obligation to honor their memory, that previous history makes the new generation stronger, and all service is for the greater good of the Country and the Academy.

THE CORPS [27]

The Corps, The Corps, The Corps

The Corps bareheaded, salute it
With eyes up thanking our God
That we of the corps are treading
Where they of the corps have trod

They are here in ghostly assemblage
The men of the corps long dead
And our hearts are standing attention
While we wait for their passing tread

We sons of today, we salute you
You sons of an earlier day
We follow close order behind you
Where you have pointed the way

The long grey line of us stretches
Through the years of a century told
And the last man feels to his marrow
The grip of your far off hold

---

27 Robert Lamb, Jane Reilly, and Barbara Sanders, eds. Bugle Notes '96, vol. 88 (West Point, NY: 1996), 287-88.

Grip hands with us now, though we see not
Grip hands with us strengthen our hearts
As the long line stiffens and straightens
With the thrill that your presence imparts

Grip hands, though it be from the shadows
While we swear as you did of yore
Or living or dying to honor
The Corps, and The Corps, and The Corps

—Bishop H.S. Shipman, Chaplain, USMA, 1896-1905

Feeling like you are constantly in the presence of all those who came before you and that you have a duty to live up to their expectations does not go away once you graduate from the Academy. In fact, I think it gets even stronger. Being a part of one of the most famous regiments in the history of the US Army is no small undertaking and brings with it a lot of pressure to perform.

The US 7th Cavalry Regiment has a very distinguished place in the annals of military history. To most people the 7th Cavalry is synonymous with Lt. Col. George Armstrong Custer and the massacre at the Little Big Horn in 1876 during the Indian Wars. The other most recognized time in history associated with the Regiment is the Battle of the Ia Drang—Landing Zone (LZ) X-Ray/Albany in November 1965 at the beginning of the Vietnam War.

Custer was the forefather of the 7th Cavalry legend, even in gruesome and notorious defeat, as he introduced the identification of "The Fighting Seventh" and "Garryowen" with the Regiment, which is still very much alive today.[28] Lt. Gen. Moore was once asked what leader he would most want to spend time with from long ago and his answer was,

---

28 The History Channel, "First in Battle: The True Story of the 7th Cavalry," (2002).

"Custer! He failed and I would like to go back over his every decision and learn directly from him what he would do differently."[29] More recently the book *We Were Soldiers Once…and Young* by retired Lt. Gen. Hal Moore and Joe Galloway in 1992 reacquainted us with this noteworthy unit. What is lost amongst these two historic periods in the Regiment's history are all the other great contributions it has made to the Nation.

While stationed at West Point, I reflected on this history (Custer is buried in the West Point cemetery) and on the remarks of Lt. Gen. Moore a great deal. I never imagined, as a young Plebe, that one day I would be back on the grounds of my rockbound highland home amongst the "ghostly assemblage" looking back and realizing I was actually an integral part of history. I never would have believed anyone sitting in my cadet history classes that the department adage of, "Much of the history we teach was made by people we taught" would ever apply to me. Before my small piece of history, however, the 7th Cavalry Regiment had already made a name for itself.

In the early years, beginning with the conclusion of the Civil War, the 7th Cavalry Regiment was a notable participant in the Indian Wars. From 1866 to 1890, the Regiment was involved at the Little Big Horn (1876) and Wounded Knee (1890), as well as various other campaigns.[30] There was a period of provost duty in Cuba from 1899-1902 and time spent fighting in the Philippine-American War on two separate occasions 1904-1907 and 1911-1915.[31] Culminating the early year's period was border patrol duty during Brigadier General John J. "Blackjack" Pershing's Mexican Expedition (Punitive Expedition) against Mexican rebel Pancho Villa in 1916-1917.[32] At the battle of Guerrero, the 7th

---

29 Moore, 19.
30 Seventh United States Cavalry Association, "Seventh United States Cavalry Unit History," http://us7thcavalry.com/7-cav-regiment-historyIndex.htm.
31 The History Channel.
32 Ibid.

Cavalry had the distinguished privilege to conduct the last true cavalry charge by a US Army unit.[33]

Throughout the inter-war period, between World War I and World War II, "the Regiment held the line as one of the last bastions of the horse cavalry" at Fort Bliss.[34] Two members of the Regiment during those times were George S. Patton Jr., A Troop Commander, and Creighton A. Abrams, F Troop who would both go on to have two of the most legendary Army careers of all time.[35] Shortly after the Great War, the 7th Cavalry Regiment would begin its affiliation with the 1st Cavalry Division (1CD); an association that part of the Regiment still has today. With the onset of World War II, the US War Department decided that the 1CD, which included the 7th Cavalry, would have to finally give up their horses.[36] This reorganization happened in February 1943 before the Division joined General (Gen.) MacArthur in the Pacific Theater.[37]

While fighting in the Pacific Theater against the Japanese, the Regiment participated in the New Guinea Campaign, as well as the Philippines Campaign between 1943 and 1945.[38] In the Philippines, the Regiment fought in the Battle of Manila, February-March 1945.[39] The 7th Cavalry also took part in the Admiralty Islands Campaign, seeing action on the islands of Negros, Hauwei, and Manus.[40]

The 7th Cavalry concluded their participation in World War II as part of the occupation force in Japan. 2nd Squadron (renamed a battalion in the future) served as the honor guard and escort for Gen. MacAr-

---

33 Seventh US Cavalry Association.
34 Ibid.
35 Ibid.
36 Ibid.
37 Ibid.
38 Ibid.
39 Thomas M. Huber, "The Battle of Manila," in *Block by Block: The Challenges of Urban Operations*, ed. William G. Robertson and Lawrence A. Yates (Fort Leavenworth, KS: U.S. Army Command and General Staff College Press, 2003), 98.
40 Seventh US Cavalry Association.

thur as he took up residence in Tokyo.[41] The unit remained in Japan until
the outbreak of the Korean War in 1950. Of note during this period the
unit transitioned from the infantry-cavalry hybrid of World War II to
a completely infantry organization, however, they retained their cavalry
designation (still called a cavalry unit despite actually being infantry).[42]

The Korean War saw part of the Regiment participate in the Pusan
Perimeter Breakout and conduct the longest advance through enemy
territory of the war.[43] Task Force 777 (3-7 CAV; C Battery, 77th Field
Artillery Battalion (FA BN); 79th Tank BN) covered a distance of 116
miles.[44] Other units of the Regiment helped seize the capital of North
Korea, Pyongyang, and went on to capture the port of Chimnampo.[45]
After the communist counter-offensive, the Regiment continued to
serve throughout the stalemate of the last two years of the war along the
39th Parallel.

I spent two years stationed in Seoul, South Korea on the Eighth
Army staff and visiting the Demilitarized Zone (DMZ) along the 39th
Parallel was an inspiring and stirring connection with the history of the
7th Cavalry Regiment. Knowing that sixty years later I was forward deployed to keep the same precarious peace they fought so hard to secure
back in 1953 was beyond special. To be able to share that experience
with my wife, Charley, and my oldest son, Caden, is a memory I will
consider one of the most extraordinary of my life.

The end of the Korean War also saw the end of the 7th Cavalry Regiment, at least for a while. Under General Order 89, Eighth Army Headquarters, dated 23 September 1957, the 24th Infantry was reflagged the
1st Cavalry Division.[46] The Army reassigned, transferred, and dispersed

---

41 The History Channel.
42 Seventh US Cavalry Association.
43 Ibid.
44 Ibid.
45 Ibid.
46 Ibid.

members of the Regiment with the reflagging to other units on 29 June 1957.[47] The 7th Cavalry Regiment would not resurface again until 1963.

The reason for all the reorganization was to form what was termed the "Pentomic Division" in 1958 to help infantry units survive and fight on the atomic battlefield.[48] The Army organized these divisions in subunits of five, each with five self-contained battle groups under its command.[49] The reorganization to form these Pentomic Divisions was the impetus that broke up the 7th Cavalry Regiment back in 1957 and when the traditional regimental and battalion organizations were eliminated.[50] There were too many concerns about the new Pentomic force design, such as span of control, organization, and leadership structure, which caused the US Army to reorganize again from 1961-1963.[51] Battle Group 1-7 was redesignated 1st Battalion, 7th Cavalry.[52] At the same time, the 11th Air Assault (Test) Division was experimenting with air mobility operations using helicopters and assumed the colors of the 1st Cavalry Division (Airmobile) in mid-1965 at Fort Benning, Georgia.[53] This was the beginning of a soon to be very historic relationship.

Fort Benning is another special place for me. My daddy grew up just to the east of Fort Benning; a small town called Thomaston and I spent a lot of time there growing up and visiting my grandparents (I was actually born in Macon, GA and lived in Thomaston before moving to Western North Carolina). As a kid, it was the only Army post I knew anything about and, to this day, I still love every minute of the sweltering heat, humidity, clay dirt, and pine trees of west Georgia. Call me crazy, but I

---

47 Ibid.

48 John M. McGrath, "Chapter 6: The Early Modern Brigade, 1958-1972," in *The Brigade: A History, Its Organization and Employment in the US Army* (Fort Leavenworth, KS: Combat Studies Institute Press, 2004), 59.

49 Ibid.

50 Ibid.

51 Ibid., 61.

52 Seventh US Cavalry Association.

53 McGrath, 64.

consider it my second home. I graduated from Airborne School there in 1998, Ranger School in 2001, and did a duty assignment to the US Army Maneuver Center of Excellence. Lt. Gen. Moore passed away and was laid to rest in the Fort Benning cemetery while I was stationed there in 2017. A very sad occurrence, but I was grateful to be present during that time. Nevertheless, enough reminiscing for now let us get back to Garryowen history...

The Vietnam War involved three of the Regiment's Battalions. 1st, 2nd, and eventually 5th were all a part of 3rd BDE, 1CD and rightly referred to as the "Garryowen Brigade".[54] After graduating from West Point in 2000, the Field Artillery Officer Basic Course, and Ranger School, I served for almost eight years in 3rd BDE, 1CD. This amount of time in one unit was unheard of back then. I considered myself fortunate and privileged to have had this honor. It gave me enough time to truly develop a significant bond with the unit and really care about it. This was no transitory passing of just a few years. This fact, plus the blood, sweat, and tears shed on behalf of the Brigade in defense of the Nation during that time has endeared itself to me very deeply.

Units from the 7th Cavalry Regiment saw action in Vietnam from 1965 through 1973. The Regiment's units distinguished themselves in the Ia Drang Valley, during the Pleiku Campaign, throughout actions in both Binh Thaun and Binh Dinh Provinces, the relief of the siege on Khe Sanh, fighting in the A Shau Valley, in and around Bien Hoa, in the Cambodian "Fish Hook" Campaign, and in the Battle of Hue.[55]

Distinguished actions, however, are not always associated with successful missions or battles. At LZ Albany in the Ia Drang Valley, 1965, my future battalion, 2-7 CAV, was caught in a very bad situation, but managed to perform valiantly and turn that situation around, unlike Custer and his troopers in 1876. Mr. Jim Lawrence (author of *Reflections*

---

54 Seventh US Cavalry Association.
55 Ibid.

on *LZ Albany: The Agony of Vietnam*), D Company, 2-7 CAV, Executive Officer (XO), described the engagement at LZ Albany in these words:

2/7 relieved 1/7 on X-Ray on Tuesday, 11/16, experienced a few probes the night of the 16th, and awoke on Wednesday, 11/17, with orders to move overland to LZ Albany. We (the men on the ground) understood that the move was necessary to get away from Chu Pong Mountain so that the B-52's from Guam could drop ordnance on the mountain. The move was not an orderly move, nor was it conducted in a tactical manner. We were tired, hungry, and assumed that the enemy had been destroyed by 1/7. We thought that we were to be air lifted out of Albany and returned to base camp. Our guard was down. It just so happened that we were moving directly towards the 8th Bn, 66th Reg, the 1st Bn, 33rd Reg, and the 3rd Bn, 33rd Reg. of regular PAVN [People's Army of Vietnam] troops. They set up an ambush, we walked into it, and they sprang it at approximately 1:15PM on Wednesday, Nov. 17. As Joe Galloway called it, "the most savage one-day battle of the Vietnam war had just begun." To put Albany in perspective, 1/7 in 2 and 1/2 days on X-Ray had 79 killed; 2/7 in about 6 hours sustained 155 KIA [killed in action]. The two LZ battles were quite different. 1/7 went into X-Ray expecting to find the enemy and fought off of an established LZ. There were no real surprises. Conversely, 2/7 was stretched out over a mile, did not expect to find opposition, and was surprised by the ambush. However, the American soldiers in each unit fought valiantly, with a very high kill ratio in favor of the Americans. Yes, we had air superiority and, yes, we had artillery, but we were fighting a well-trained, determined foe and, in the case of Albany, an enemy who had the element of surprise on their side. Yet we not only survived, but prevailed. No, it did not feel like a "victory" because we lost a lot of very good men; as has been written many times, the cost of victory is high. Apparently, the encounters on the two LZs in the Ia Drang caused the North Vietnamese to alter their strategy; to avoid face-to-face confrontations with large units, which they could not win, but to use smaller unit, hit-and-run tactics so prevalent later in the war. Looking back, mistakes were made on Albany, but the American fighting man on the ground overcame those mistakes and demonstrated a spirit consistent with our military legacy.[56]

Another member of the battalion, Private First Class (Pfc.) Jack P. Smith recounted events at LZ Albany during a speech to the Ia Drang Survivors Banquet 8 November 2003 in Crystal City, Virginia. Mr. Smith told the audience,

I came in on the last day of the battle. I remember the NVA [North Vietnamese Army, synonymous with PAVN] bodies were piled so thick around the foxholes you could walk on them for 100 feet in some places. The American GIs [Soldiers] were the same color as the dirt and all had that thousand-yard stare of those newly initiated to combat. The next day, after a restless night, my battalion, the 2/7, walked away from X-ray toward another clearing called LZ Albany. Around lunchtime, we were jumped by a North Vietnamese formation. Like us, about 500-strong. The fighting was hand-to-hand. I was lying so close to a North Vietnamese machine-gunner that I simply stuck out my rifle and blew off his head. It was, I think, the only time during the war that a U.S. battalion was ever overrun. The U.S. casualties for this fourth day of battle: 155 killed, 121 wounded. More dead than wounded. The North Vietnamese suffered a couple of hundred casualties… The ferocity of the fighting during those four days was appalling.

---

56 Jim Lawrence, April 2012.

At one point in the awful afternoon at Albany, as my battalion was being cut to pieces, a small group of enemy came upon me, and thinking I had been killed (I was covered in other people's blood), proceeded to use me as a sandbag for their machine gun. I pretended to be dead. I remember the gunner had bony knees that pressed against my sides. He didn't discover I was alive because he was trembling more than I was. He was, like me, just a teenager. The gunner began firing into the remnants of my company. My buddies began firing back with rifle grenades, M-79s, to those of you who know about them. I remember thinking, "Oh, my God. If I stand up, the North Vietnamese will kill me; and if I stay lying down, my buddies will get me." Before I went completely mad, a volley of grenades exploded on top of me, killing the enemy boy and injuring me. It went on like this all day and much of the night. I was wounded twice and thought myself dead. My company suffered about 93 percent casualties—93 percent... This sort of experience leaves scars. I had nightmares. For years afterwards, I was sour on life, by turns angry, cynical, and alienated... I have discovered that wounds heal. That the friendship of old comrades breathes meaning into life. And that even the most disjointed events can begin to make sense with the passage of time. This has allowed me, on evenings like this, to step forward and take pride in the service I gave my country. But never to forget what was, and will always be, the worst day of my life. The day I escaped death in the tall grass of the Ia Drang Valley.[57]

Units of the 1st Cavalry Division served throughout the Vietnam War. They were some of the first to arrive and some of the last to with-

---

57 Jack P. Smith, "Sandbag for a Machine Gun: Jack P. Smith on the Battle of the Ia Drang Valley and the Legacy of the Vietnam War," http://www.mishalov.com/death_ia_drang_valley.html.

draw. Then there was a relative quiet period for the Regiment between Vietnam and military involvement in the Middle East.

When the situation in the Persian Gulf escalated to the point of requiring military action, however, the Regiment was there. Two battalions of the 7th Cavalry saw action in the Gulf War. 1st and 4th Battalions participated in the liberation of Kuwait from Iraqi forces in 1991.[58] The most intense action seen by either battalion was the Battle of Phase Line Bullet by 4-7 CAV, which often goes unnoticed in the long history of valorous conduct by the Regiment. [59] Once again, however, members of The Fighting Seventh did a superb job in the face of the enemy, distinguishing themselves as can only be expected from a Garryowen battalion.

Most recently, Garryowen units have seen action in the Iraq War. 3-7 CAV, as a member of 3rd Infantry Division, was integral in the "March Up" during the initial invasion of Iraq in 2003, culminating with the fall of Baghdad. Other 7th Cavalry battalions, 1-7 CAV, 2-7 CAV, and 5-7 CAV subsequently deployed with various rotations of OIF until the conclusion of the war in 2011. 2-7 CAV Ghost, in addition, notably distinguished themselves in two of the most high-profile battles of the post-invasion war, in both Najaf and Fallujah, Operation Phantom Fury (Al Fajr-Arabic for New Dawn) or just the Second Battle of Fallujah.

Bestowed unit decorations well document the actions of the Regiment and its Battalions throughout their history. I will highlight just a few to give you an inkling of the massive contribution of all that have served as part of the 7th Cavalry. The Presidential Unit Citation (PUC) is the highest unit award given in any service for a unit displaying "such gallantry, determination, and esprit de corps in accomplishing its mission under extremely difficult and hazardous conditions as to set it apart

---

58 Seventh US Cavalry Association.
59 The History Channel.

from and above other units participating in the same campaign."[60] The
degree of heroism by the unit is equivalent to the personal award of the
Distinguished Service Cross (one level below the Medal of Honor).[61]

A unit earns the Valorous Unit Award when they have shown val-
or corresponding to the individual award of the Silver Star along with
the Navy Unit Commendation (NUC) for extraordinary or outstanding
heroism just short of the PUC.[62] Units exhibiting the gallantry akin to
the personal award of the Legion of Merit earn the Army Meritorious
Unit Commendation.[63]

Units of the 7th Cavalry have earned every single one of these on
multiple occasions, except the Navy Unit Commendation, which has
only been awarded once.[64] 2-7 CAV earned the NUC for its participation with the 1st Marine Division (1MARDIV) in the Second Battle
of Fallujah in November 2004. For that same action, 2-7 CAV also received the PUC. This was one of only seven awarded during the Iraq War
(2003-2011).[65] My 2-7 CAV was not just successful because it won battles, but because the members that made it up were some great leaders.
I saw and experienced much of Lt. Gen. Moore's leadership influence
while serving in the Ghost Battalion. It almost seemed like 2-7 CAV
circa 2004 was destined to play a significant role based upon our name,
our quality, and the volatile situation of the time.

---

60 US Department of the Army, *Army Regulation 600-8-22*, 2015, 82.

61 Ibid.

62 Ibid., 83; US Department of the Navy, "Navy Unit Commendation
(NU)," https://awards.navy.mil/awards/webapp01.nsf/(vwAwardsDisp)/AW-
10052085MQQS?OpenDocument.

63 Army, 84.

64 Seventh United States Cavalry Association, "Seventh United States Cavalry Unit
Decorations," http://us7thcavalry.com/7-cav-Reg-Decorations.htm.

65 Richard K. Kolb, Tim Dyhouse, and Janie Blankenship, "Heroes of Iraq," *VFW*,
March 2012, 19.

4. DESTINY

The hardship of the exercises is intended less to strengthen the back than to toughen the mind. The Spartans say that any army may win while it still has its legs under it; the real test comes when all strength is fled and the men must produce victory on will alone.

—Steven Pressfield, *Gates of Fire*

Great units cannot very well achieve the recognition and stature of a historic unit without first proving itself in the arena in which it was created to perform. For an Army mechanized infantry battalion like 2-7 CAV, that arena is war. It is the ultimate evaluation of both the unit and the individuals of which it is comprised. 2-7 CAV of 2004 knew the 7th Cavalry had proved itself in the past, we knew they were one of America's best, we knew they had been led by some of America's finest, and the question going through our minds before Fallujah was, "How do we fit in? What will be our legacy? Will this be our crucible test that will elevate us to the same level of prominence as the unit to which we owed our identity?"

We know now that Fallujah turned out to be a defining moment for the 7th Cavalry. Looking back, The Second Battle of Fallujah would be the single deadliest occurrence of US losses due to enemy action in the Iraq War (2003-2011)[66] How did we get there? Planned? Partly so, maybe... For a hopeless romantic like me, could it have been destiny? I can believe

---

66 Richard K. Kolb and Kelly Von Lunen, "Iraq War Casualties," *VFW* 2012, 58.

it. The Second Battle of Fallujah, described as "one of the most decisive urban victories our nation has ever seen" by Col. Michael Shupp, Commander of Regimental Combat Team — 1 (RCT-1), 1MARDIV, 1st Marine Expeditionary Force (MEF), United States Marine Corps (USMC), was not an anomaly in our history.[67] If you heed Lt. Gen. Moore's advice, dig back through history, and read military history, you quickly realize the Regiment had been in a similar spot before.[68] The Battle of Manila, 3 February through 3 March 1945, was the only fight to seize a major defended city in the Pacific Theater and only one of a few major urban battles in all of World War II.[69] Involved in that fight was none other than the 7th Cavalry Regiment as part of the 1st Cavalry Division.

They only played a small role, which is not too bad for a bunch of horse soldiers that just gave up their mounts a few years before. The small role they did play, however, held quite a bit of importance. Gen. Walter Krueger, 6th Army Commander, assigned them the critical task to preserve as much of the city functions and utilities to aid in the administration of the city after its capture. The securing and protection of the city's water system fell to the 1st Cavalry Division and the 7th Cavalry Regiment.[70] The 7th Cavalry captured all these facilities intact between 5 and 8 February 1945 and safeguarded them for the rest of the battle.[71]

A few decades later, the 7th Cavalry participated in one of the most famous battles in American history and especially of the Vietnam War. The Battle of Hue, 1968 is a household name spoken by several generations in the same breath as Ia Drang, Hamburger Hill, A Shau, and Khe Sanh. An arduous counteroffensive in response to the Tet Offensive, Hue presented some difficult problems. As the ancient capital of Vietnam and a sacred spot to Buddhists, American forces had to expel

---

67 Michael Shupp, interview by Matt Matthews, March 25, 2006, 66.
68 Cole C. Kingseed, "Beyond the Ia Drang Valley," *Army Magazine*, November 2002, 22.
69 Huber, 91.
70 Ibid., 98.
71 Ibid.

North Vietnamese forces (PAVN or NVA) without total destruction of the city or face large-scale political repercussions.[72] These trends (in Manila and Hue) would resurface in another century with a new generation of American warriors in a similar predicament.

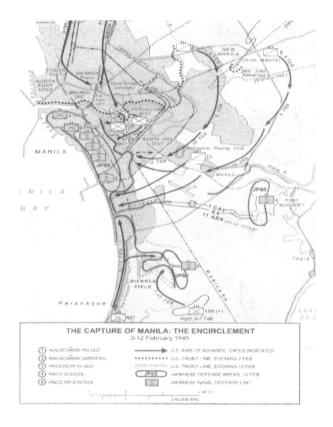

Source: Huber, Thomas M. "The Battle of Manila." In *Block by Block: The Challenges of Urban Operations,* edited by William G. Robertson and Lawrence A. Yates, 91-122. Fort Leavenworth, KS: US Army Command and General Staff College Press, 2003.

Hue was primarily a Marine mission, but planning identified the need for reinforcements. One of the units chosen was 3rd BDE, 1CD.

---

72 James H. Willbanks, "The Battle of Hue, 1968," ibid. (US Army Command and General Staff College Press), 136.

Their mission was to block enemy approaches into the city from the north and west, essentially isolating the city for the Marines and South Vietnamese forces (ARVN, Army of the Republic of Vietnam) forces to retake Hue.[73] Throughout the month of February 1968, 1-7 and 5-7 CAV faced stiff resistance on the outskirts of Hue with the help of 2-12 CAV and 2-501st Infantry (IN), blocking PAVN movement and inhibiting their participation in the violent clash in Hue itself.[74]

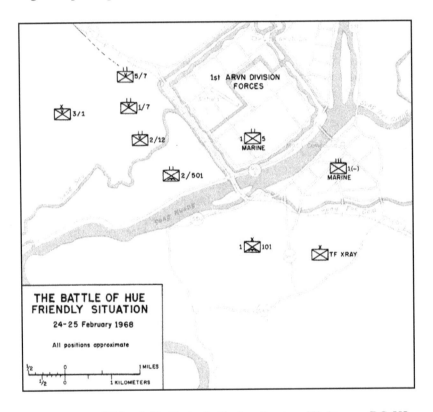

Source: Pearson, Williard. *The War in the Northern Provinces.* Washington, DC: US Government Printing Office, 1975. Accessed March 9, 2012. http://www.history.army. mil/books/Vietnam/norther/nprovinces.htm.

---

73 Ibid.
74 Ibid., 137.

Another joint operation (multiple services fighting together) in an urban environment with Marines came 36 years later in Najaf, Iraq, 2004 during the Iraq War. This time 2-7 CAV served as the representative from the Regiment. Throughout the summer, Muqtatda al-Sadr, an important Shia Cleric, and his Mahdi Militia continued to increase resistance to the new Interim Iraqi Government (IIG) causing problems in Baghdad and elsewhere in the country. At the same time, 2-7 CAV was bringing onboard a new battalion chain of command. The two Majors, the XO and Operations Officer (S3), moved on to follow-on assignments as part of normal officer turnover. The Command Sergeant Major (Command Sgt. Maj.) was also re-assigned and it was time for a new battalion commander (BN CDR) as well. The new leadership would prove very influential and instrumental in both Najaf and later operations. The ability to lead effectively so soon after key personnel transitions before a major operation like Najaf was evidence of the great character of the members of the battalion.

The resistance by Sadr and his militia continued to progress to the point of open conflict in Najaf late in the summer of 2004 and the 11th Marine Expeditionary Unit (MEU) requested reinforcements to deal with the uprising. They requested these forces through the Multi-National Forces-Iraq (MNF-I) Commander, Gen. George W. Casey, who in turn tasked the 1CD to provide two battalions to help.[75] The 2nd and 39th BDEs (39th BDE from the Arkansas National Guard) were chosen to provide a battalion each; 2nd BDE provided 1-5 CAV and 39th BDE provided 2-7 CAV.[76]

2-7 CAV was an easy selection as they were serving outside the main effort of 1CD, which had responsibility for all of Baghdad. Outside the city proper, 2-7 CAV operated from Taji — north of Baghdad, and therefore was considered an economy of force mission that was not as critical

---

75 Richard D. Camp, *Battle for the City of the Dead: In the Shadow of the Golden Dome, Najaf, August 2004* (Minneapolis, MN: Zenith Press, 2011), 151.
76 Ibid., 151-53.

to the progress of the war. Senior leaders felt they could afford to send 2-7 CAV to support the fight in Najaf. The so-called "Battle for the City of the Dead", coined by author Dick Camp, proved pivotal to planning for the Second Battle of Fallujah. Marines and Soldiers learned many lessons that would be applied later in the year on an even larger scale.

One of the most valuable outcomes of Najaf was the opportunity to earn a reputation and build rapport between two services that are very competitive with one another. Maj. Tim Karcher, 2-7 CAV S3, recalls,

> *The fact that we did* some pretty robust destruction for them, if you will, and killed a lot of enemy for them, we got a reputation with the 11th MEU—and thereby the 1st MEF—as a unit that could go in and mix it up with whatever the enemy had to offer...[77]

First Lieutenant (1st Lt.) Mike Erwin, 2-7 Intelligence Officer (S2), attributed the ability to provide that robust destruction to having the right attitude. He remembers that when they first arrived there was "no us showing up and expecting a certain mission or a certain role. We just showed up there and knew we were there to help them...saying we would do whatever they needed us to do, and I think that really played a big role in it."[78] By the end of the battle, it was safe to say that the Marines saw 2-7 CAV as equal fighters and warriors, an attribute highly coveted by the Marine Corps. Lt. Col. Jim Rainey, 2-7 BN CDR, knew the reason for those compliments by the Marines and summed it up, simply stating that the outcome of Najaf and the battalion's performance was due primarily "[to] young leaders and noncommissioned officers."[79]

The Battle of Najaf not only improved inter-service camaraderie, but it was tremendously important to the battalion's confidence and trust

---

77 Tim Karcher, interview by Matt Matthews, March 14, 2006, 199.
78 Michael S. Erwin, interview by Matt Matthews, April 19, 2006, 49.
79 James Rainey, interview by Matt Matthews, April 19, 2006, 111.

among team members. After going through necessary leadership turn-over and then being thrust into a challenging tactical situation, there was much for the battalion to gain from the experience. Captain (Capt.) Chris Brooke, Charlie Company Commander (C/2-7 CO CDR-Co-manche 6), explained,

> *When it was all finished*, there was a bond of trust that spanned all the way from the battalion leadership down to the individual soldier and from the individual soldier, all the way back up. The officers and soldiers alike would follow Lt. Colonol Rainey any-where. Most important of all, the soldiers trusted each other.[80]

Command Sgt. Maj. Tim Mace, 2-7 senior non-commissioned offi-cer (Ghost 9), understood, "The soldiers were battle hardened by Najaf," which would prepare them for later in Fallujah, "basically Najaf on a more vicious scale."[81]

At this point, from a historical perspective all that needed to happen to reach a new pinnacle in military history was: 1) for an urban operation to take place on a grander scale than Hue; 2) the operation needed to be the biggest battle of a war (with Marine and Army units in combat side by side); and 3) for a nation's potential destiny to be hanging in the balance based upon the outcome. That perfect storm of events would manifest themselves two months later in the City of Mosques just 30-40 miles west of Baghdad, in Fallujah. Who would be some of those indi-viduals destined to make such important history?

---

80 Chris Brooke, interview by Matt Matthews, May 1, 2006, 267.
81 Timothy L. Mace, interview by Matt Matthews, April 19, 2006, 186.

5. GHOSTS

The Spartans have a term for that state of mind which must at all costs be shunned in battle. They call it *katalepsis*, possession, meaning that derangement of the senses that comes when terror or anger usurps dominion of the mind. This, I realized now watching Dienekes rally and tend to his men, was the role of the officer: to prevent those under his command, at all stages of the battle—before, during and after—from becoming "possessed." To fire their valor when it flagged and rein in their fury when it threatened to take them out of hand…He was not a superhuman who waded invulnerably into the slaughter, single-handedly slaying the foe by myriads. He was just a man doing a job. A job whose primary attribute was self-restraint and self-composure, not for his own sake, but for those whom he led by his example.[82]

—Steven Pressfield, *Gates of Fire*

The military is all about people. Leading and soldiering is a people business. 2-7 CAV was no different. We had many great people, bottom to top. Our battalion in the hands of our excellent leaders was an overwhelming and unrelenting force. Our people were absolutely the best. The easiest decision in the world was putting your trust and well-being in the hands of those around you in the Ghost Battalion. In the next few

---

82 Pressfield, 112.

pages, I am going to introduce you to some of the Ghosts of 2-7 CAV that played a fundamental and essential role in the Second Battle of Fallujah. Men that I witnessed in action first hand, some of those next generation leaders that carried on in the "Garryowen" tradition. Men that would make Lt. Gen. Moore proud and men I learned a lot from, which had a personal impact on my life through their words, deeds, and actions.

THE BRASS

Col. Michael Shupp, USMC, was our Regimental Commander, Inchon 6, during the Second Battle of Fallujah. He is one of two honorary Ghosts that I will introduce in this chapter. I cannot imagine a better fit for a brigade/regimental commander for a unit like ours. Within moments of meeting him, you knew he was cut from the same cloth as the warriors of 2-7 CAV. His demeanor, mannerisms, and attitude demanded instant respect. He exhibited an aura that radiated a "can do" spirit. You just knew you could not fail with him at the helm. Col. Shupp was a leader that Marines and Soldiers would follow to the ends of the earth. He was born in Bethlehem, Pennsylvania and graduated from the Virginia Military Institute in 1981.[83] Before becoming the commander of Regimental Combat Team 1 (RCT-1), Col. Shupp, held many jobs in the USMC and had prior experience in the Middle East as a company commander during the Gulf War.[84]

My Battalion Commander, Lt. Col. James "Jim" Rainey, Ghost 6, and School of Advanced Military Studies (SAMS) graduate was an imposing figure of a man that was always a bit intimidating to me. Always a coffee in hand, with dip and gum in his mouth, he looked the part of a rough and tumble fighter that you just did not mess with. Lt. Col. Rainey was a tough love leader who set high expectations for his officers

---

83 Shupp, 2006, 47.
84 Ibid.

and Soldiers, but none that were not attainable. His example set the tone for how he expected the battalion to act and be. Simply put, follow him, and do as he did. Lt. Col. Rainey was always on the ground, leading from the front, and you could tell by looking into his eyes he was in constant thought about what was going on. He was born in Brockton, Massachusetts, however he grew up in Akron, Ohio.[85] Lt. Col. Rainey was commissioned out of Eastern Kentucky University in 1987 and on his way to battalion command; he served in the 82nd Airborne Division, 75th Ranger Regiment, 3rd Infantry Regiment (Old Guard), and the 1st Cavalry Division as a company commander, S3 for 1-9 CAV, and 3rd BDE XO.[86]

Col. Shupp, Commander RCT-1 (left)
and Lt. Col. Rainey, Commander 2-7 CAV (right)
Source: Matthews, Matt. *Operation Al Fajr: A Study in Army and Marine Corps Joint Operations.* Fort Leavenworth, KS: Combat Studies Institute, 2006.

---

85 Rainey, 2006, 109.
86 Ibid.

Maj. Tim Karcher, Ghost 3, and SAMS graduate was a perfect fit
for the unit. When I think back about Maj. Karcher, there is the feeling
that you are standing in front of a modern day cowboy. Hard working,
always down on the ground willing to do the dirty work, and not afraid
of a good fight. A big fan of a good cigar; you could always count on one
being close by if not clinched between his teeth. Maj. Karcher was another true warrior with an excellent mind, like so many of the members
of our battalion. This mix was a dangerous combination for any enemy,
an exceptionally smart and lethal combatant. Maj. Karcher graduated
from the University of Missouri, Columbia in 1989 and commissioned
through the Reserve Officers'Training Corps (ROTC).[87] Before arriving
at 2-7 CAV, Maj. Karcher, spent time at the National Training Center
as Opposing Forces (enemy role players for units to train against), held
two company commands, and taught tactics at the Infantry School and
Advanced Course.[88]

Maj. Scott Jackson, Ghost 5, and SAMS graduate, entered the United States Army upon receiving a commission as a Second Lieutenant
(2nd Lt.) and graduation from the University of Notre Dame.[89] As our
XO and second in command, Maj. Jackson had to be ready at any time
to step in and lead the battalion, as well as ensure the staff supported
battalion operations properly. One of his primary duties was responsibility for all staff sections: Personnel (S1), Intelligence (S2), Supply (S4),
Civil Military Operations (S5), Communications (S6), Fires, and the
Rear Detachment back home. He had an uncanny knack for efficient
management of the myriad of tasks belonging to numerous staff sections
and getting all those personnel working together. For the most part re-
served, solemn, and quiet, I knew that Maj. Jackson was all business. He
was a thinker, exceptionally bright, and it seemed nothing took him by
surprise. When he spoke, I listened because he always had something

---

87 Karcher, 2006, 199.
88 Ibid.
89 Scott Jackson, "Linkedin Profile," LinkedIn.

important to say that warranted my attention. I learned a lot from him, not just about the tactical mission, but also the other crucial responsibilities the battalion had back home.

Command Sgt. Maj. Timothy Mace, Ghost 9, was an old school and very seasoned Soldier. He looked the part as well. He had a great sense of humor and always knew the exact right moments when some wit was just what the doctor ordered. He was the non-commissioned officer (NCO) every officer wished they could have working with them for their entire career. A wealth of knowledge and a no bullshit kind of leader; you would be hard pressed to find a better right hand man. Command Sgt. Maj. Mace was born in St. Louis, Missouri in 1960 and joined the Army in June 1978.[90] An infantryman through and through, from beginning to end, he followed the light infantryman's career path: Basic Training, Advanced Individual Training, Airborne School, then off to Italy (airborne unit), then Ft. Campbell (Air Assault Instructor), then Ft. Bragg (airborne unit), Drill Instructor, and then Ft. Bragg some more.[91] He finally ended up in a heavy mechanized infantry unit, his first one, but it did not unnerve him in the least. Leading Soldiers was leading Soldiers for him, anytime, anywhere.

THE COMMANDERS

If "The Brass" were like fathers to me, then "The Commanders" were like big brothers. They had all served their staff time, had been selected for and were now serving in what is likely considered the greatest duty position an officer can ever hold...company command. I knew to pay attention to how they commanded and operated because not too long down the road that could be me. If I was lucky, it would be me, and in combat...one of the truest tests of an officer.

---

90 Mace, 2006, 185.
91 Ibid.

Capt. Ed Twaddell, Alpha CO CDR (A/2-7), Apache 6, was a 1997 graduate of West Point and native of Jaffrey, New Hampshire.[92] He served in the 101st Airborne before showing up at the 1st Cavalry Division and worked his way down to the battalion from 3rd BDE Headquarters as an Assistant Operations officer (A/S3),* taking command of Apache Company in November 2003.[93] Ed always struck me as particularly mature; he looked a bit older than his peers and seemed well suited to the military profession. Upon meeting him, you immediately experienced a sense of calm and trust as he exuded competence on every level. You knew there was nothing that he or his company could not handle.

Capt. Chris Brooke, Charlie CO CDR (C/2-7), Comanche 6, was the newest commander in the battalion. He was born in San Antonio, Texas and was a graduate of Texas A&M University.[94] Chris's first assignment was with the 25th Infantry Division before he arrived at 2-7 CAV as an A/S3 prior to taking command of Comanche Company in October 2004, just one month before the Second Battle of Fallujah.[95] I remember he spent the most time of all the commanders talking with the junior captains on the staff. He was always very friendly and voraciously sought all information that he could get his hands on that might affect his company. As the newest commander, I watched him closely for the lessons learned by the new guy on the block.

Capt. Pete Glass "Capt. Chaos" or Cougar 6, was the CO CDR for Charlie Company, 3rd Battalion, 8th Cavalry (3-8 CAV) which was task organized (temporarily assigned) to our battalion to give us an ar-

---

92 Edward Twaddell, interview by Matt Matthews, February 28, 2006, 125; McAllester, "Guerilla's Paradise," 4.
93 Twaddell, 2006, 125.

* Note: In combat, A/S3s are called and serve as "Battle Captains." They are the Commander's representative in the Tactical Operations Center and manage battle tracking, communications, and initiate battalion level first response (e.g. quick reaction force deployment) to troops on the ground in need of reinforcement.
94 Brooke, 2006, 263.
95 Ibid.

mor (tank) capability. Pete was an Army "brat" whose father served for 29 years.[96] He was born in Schaumburg, Illinois and was a graduate of The Citadel's ROTC program in Charleston, South Carolina.[97] He was commissioned as an infantry officer, served at Ft. Stewart, Georgia, and Ft. Bragg with the XVIII Airborne Corp to include a deployment to Afghanistan.[98] On his way to company command in 3-8 CAV, he branch transferred to the Armor Branch. Capt. Glass was a natural "tanker" and performed his duties as if he had been doing it his whole life. Pete always displayed a contagious air of confidence, boldness, and daring that made you want to forget immediately what you were doing and join him on his latest adventure. He needed very little guidance before you could cut him loose to accomplish any mission you gave him.

Capt. Jake Brown held the tough job of being our Forward Support Company (FSC) Commander. He commanded Bravo Company, 215th Forward Support Battalion, assigned to support 2-7 CAV. All mechanized and armor forces require expert and extensive maintenance to keep them running. Not to mention the damage combat can cause on top of normal wear and tear, which makes it hard to keep vehicles in the fight. Jake and his company, in austere conditions, kept our battalion's firepower where it needed to be, in Fallujah.

Capt. Chris Chambliss was our Headquarters and Headquarters Company (HHC) Commander. He was in charge of the mortar platoon, the medic platoon, all the staff, and 2nd Platoon, Bravo Company, 2nd Battalion, 162nd Infantry (2/B/2-162 IN) who was the security force for the battalion headquarters in Fallujah (B/2-162 IN was also task organized to the battalion while in Iraq). With so many moving parts, it could be difficult to manage, but he harmoniously synchronized all those pieces in support of the battalion effort. I would later hold a HHC command (during my second deployment to Iraq) and would even better

---

96 Peter Glass, interview by Matt Matthews, March 29, 2006, 71.
97 Ibid.
98 Ibid.

understand after the fact what a tough and sometimes thankless job he did on a daily basis.

Capt. Chaos atop his tank in Fallujah
Source: Photo courtesy of Eric Hough

THE STAFF

Being a staff officer is not the most glamorous job you can have, but it does serve a very important purpose. If you do not do your job well and to a high standard, you can severely hinder the ability of the whole battalion. A battalion decisively engaged in combat operations cannot afford one weak leak, no matter how small of a leak you think it might be. The 2-7 CAV staff was truly out of this world. This staff was a talented and a tight nit team that you expected great things from in the fight and down the road in the future.

Our Personnel Officer (S1) was 1st Lt. Kyle St. Laurent who moved up to our staff from Comanche Company where he was a Platoon Leader (PL).[99] He worked closely with the Supply Officer (S4) in the Army Logistics Operations Center (ALOC) to manage the innumerable administrative duties critical in combat. His duties primarily focused on coordinating with the battalion surgeon and medical personnel for the medical service plan to include treatment areas, evacuations, and casualty affairs. I wish he would have been the least busy officer on the staff, but Fallujah would get a vote.

Capt. Sheldon Morris, our S4, was the other primary member of our ALOC. His mission was managing our logistical concerns, which meant food, ammunition, fuel, etc. Everyone knows that if the logistics are not straight, then a force is ineffective in a fight. This is especially true of a heavy mechanized force. That is why famous generals like Napoléon made statements such as, "An army marches on its stomach" and "The amateurs discuss tactics; the professionals discuss logistics." Despite many challenges during our time in Fallujah, a lack of supplies was never an issue. Capt. Morris would have impressed even the most knowledgeable military leaders of the past. Sheldon hailed from Jacksonville, Florida and attended the University of Mississippi (Ole Miss) where he participated in the ROTC program.[100] After his commissioning, he attended the Infantry Officer Basic Course, Airborne School, Ranger School, and the Bradley Leaders Course.[101] Before becoming the S4, he was the Scout Platoon Leader and XO for Comanche Company.[102] In his free time, he was an exceptional football player as our battalion flag football contests could attest.

Without communication, a military mission is doomed to failure. Capt. John Ontko was our Communications Officer (S6). He made sure in an isolated environment far from Camp Fallujah that we were always linked into the communications architecture so we could talk to higher

---

99 Brooke, 2006, 267.
100 Sheldon Morris, interview by Matt Matthews, April 23, 2006, 3.
101 Ibid.
102 Ibid.

and our Companies. John not only was able to make our equipment work, but was also able to integrate the differing systems between the Marines and Army into a functional communications network. We had the least amount of communications issues that I have seen anywhere else in my career, and we were fighting a large-scale battle where everything was supposed to go wrong.

Our intelligence section was top notch. Capt. Dave Gray (S2) and 1st Lt. Mike Erwin (A/S2) were vital to our fight in Fallujah. Both were extraordinarily sharp with the uncanny ability to decipher intelligence reports, allowing for an actionable estimate of enemy activities. Dave was a 1999 USMA graduate from Houston, Texas and Mike was a 2002 USMA graduate from Syracuse, New York (would later become a USMA leadership instructor and founder of Team Red, White, & Blue).[103] 1st Lt. Erwin decided to join Military Intelligence after 9/11 happened because he felt he could really help the war effort in that capacity.[104] I remember they were always thinking, always reading, always researching, always studying, and always trying to find another way to get ahead of the enemy to help the Soldiers on the ground. Sometimes military intelligence gets a bad "rap" and the joke is always how the term is such an oxymoron, well not these two guys! Their work was no joke and to trust their assessments and deductions was a "no-brainer."

Our A/S3s (Battle Captains in active combat, see earlier note) were both 1998 USMA graduates. Capts. Chris Conley and Pete Chapman were both serving in that staff position as the last stop on the way to their own company commands. Being a Battle Captain meant that the battalion commander had a lot of trust in your abilities to monitor, track, and direct the fight when one of the senior officers was not around. The trust to make decisions to deal with the situation until the S3, XO, or BN CDR could be briefed and further guidance rendered. A very important and stressful job in a high intensity conflict that was suit-

103 Erwin, 2006, 47.
104 Ibid.

ed for those ready for the next challenge (company command) when called upon. Chris was from Massachusetts and was a towering figure in my eyes. I always felt he could squash me like a bug anytime he wanted with his 75th Ranger Battalion experience. Pete was from Georgia, more my size and not quite so physically imposing, but exceptionally smart (would later become a USMA Physics instructor). As the senior Captains on the staff I looked up to both of them and wanted to make sure they approved of my work. They were deliberate, calm, and two very "cool cats" under pressure.

Capt. Gray (rear left), Capts. Conley and Chapman (center), Capt. Ontko (rear right with sunglasses on his head, Specialist (Spc.) Manning, and Pvt. Bown—two of my Fires Soldiers (front center)
Source: Photo courtesy of Mike Erwin

Capt. Lee "Stroker" Gentile Jr. with stylish mustache (left) and James Janega of the
Chicago Tribune (right) early in the morning, coffee in hand
Source: Photo courtesy of Michael Erwin

Capt. Lee Gentile Jr., Toxin Team Commander, and an A-10 pilot
from the United States Air Force (USAF), call sign "Stroker" was assigned
to our battalion to give us an air capability that was not normally organic to our unit. The "powers that be" however, saw fit with our upcoming
mission that the asset of Joint Terminal Attack Controllers (JTACs) led
by an Air Liaison Officer (ALO) would come in handy. To say they came
in handy is a gross understatement to be sure. Capt. Gentile was born
in Massachusetts and graduated from Worcester Polytechnic Institute in
1997 with a degree in Civil Engineering and was in the ROTC program.
Stroker epitomized the combination of a brilliant mind with a charismatic
"cool guy" magnetism. He was Maverick from *Top Gun* with the smarts
of Viper and the humor and down-to-earth family centeredness of Goose
all rolled into one. If I were a pilot, I would want him as my wingman all

the time. I, of course, was not a pilot, but in Fallujah, I was lucky to have him as my wingman in another sense. I will never forget that fashionable mustache that only an A-10 pilot could pull off either.

Finally, that brings us to myself. I was born in Georgia and grew up in Western North Carolina. I attended West Point, as you know, and graduated in 2000. I was a very lean, but fit officer that looked years younger than his age. Sometimes I wonder how anyone ever took me seriously with my baby face appearance. I was soft spoken and tended to communicate most effectively through my actions and example. One thing that could pull me out of my shell and get me quite animated and talkative was artillery, but not just any aspect of artillery.

I graduated from my Field Artillery Officer Basic Course at Ft. Sill, Oklahoma towards the top of my class, but not on the Commandant's List. I had a knack for fire support, but my lack of excitement about gunnery and gun line operations hurt my performance. I realized after six months of schooling that I was better suited for the art and creativity needed to integrate fire support into maneuver operations, much more so than the robotic and programmed, only one correct answer, specific math and science of gunnery. As a fire supporter I imagined myself being a bit of a cavalier with the ability to show a little more flamboyance and flair in my work, analogous with so many of the great leaders of the past that have captured so many imaginations. Some that come to mind are Generals Henry "Light Horse Harry" Lee, Francis "The Swamp Fox" Marion, or George "Old Blood and Guts" Patton.

After my Officer Basic Course, I spent an extended tour at the US Army Ranger School. I was a two-time recycle in both Darby (Phase I) and Mountains (Phase II) and I would not have it any other way! I learned so much more about myself, my limits, and being a Soldier than I would have if I had graduated the first time through. The two guys that taught me the most about being a Soldier were my closest Ranger buddies, John Doe (cannot be named for security resaons), 3rd Ranger Battalion and Navy Lieutenant (Lt.) Mike "Groove" McGreevy, a Navy SEAL (Sea, Air, Land-Navy Special Forces) and Class 07-01 Top Ranger (Killed in Action, 28 June 2005, Afghanistan, SEAL Team Ten). We were the baddest M240B machine gun team (gunner, assistant gunner, and ammo bearer) in the history of Ranger School if you ask me. I will never forget patrolling the woods, mountains, and swamps with those two men, humping around our machine gun, which we named "El Diablo." Interestingly, I spent so much time in Ranger School (5 months) that I was actually kicked out of the Defense Financial and Accounting Services (how you are paid in the military) because the Army thought I had gone absent without leave (AWOL). I was lost in Ranger School! I eventually made it to Ft. Hood, Texas and 3rd BDE, 1CD a few pounds lighter, a lot harder, and ready to make a difference to the "First Team." (nickname for the 1CD)

Lt. McGreevy (top row, fourth from right) and 2nd Lt. Tyler & John Doe (second row from top, sixth and seventh from the right respectively)
Source: Photo courtesy of Coley Tyler

I found myself in 2-7 CAV as a second order effect of the natural progression of officer moves driven by career progression in September of 2004. I was serving as the S2 for 2-82 FA BN "Steel Dragons" in Baghdad. 2-82 FA was also a part of the 3rd BDE Greywolf. Besides being in direct support of the maneuver battalions with indirect fires, executing our own mission as security for the Coalition Provincial Authority and the State Department, our battalion assigned officers to each battalion of the Brigade to run their Fire Support Elements (FSE). The 2-7 CAV Fire Support Officer (FSO), Capt. Greg Schrein, was up for command back in 2-82 FA and needed replacing so he could take command of his battery. The 2-82 FA BN CDR selected me to move up to Taji, just north of Baghdad where 2-7 CAV was stationed to replace him.

I was extremely nervous after being given the job, as normally that position was for more seasoned Captains that had already attended the Captains Career Course (second level of officer professional education after the Officer Basic Course, but before Intermediate Level Education for Majors) and one of the last jobs you fulfilled before taking Battery Command. I had been a Captain for just under 12 months at that point. Not only that, I was not going to just any unit, I was going to 2-7 CAV who had just become highly distinguished and renowned throughout Iraq as one of the units that had just fought the Battle of Najaf against the Mahdi Militia of Muqtada al-Sadr in August. At that point, I was very excited, but had an intense anxiety, which accompanies you when you are entering a realm with extremely high expectations, not just in the present, but also from the past. I had somehow managed to end up in 3rd BDE, 1CD, and was now headed to the 7th Cavalry doing what I was so passionate about; it was an ambition come true and I did not want to foul it up. My wildest dreams as a Plebe getting my book autographed by Lt. Gen. Moore had become a reality.

THE VOICE

Mr. Matt McAllester was one of our embedded reporters during the Battle of Fallujah. A very intelligent, articulate, and dedicated journalist, he wrote some very riveting and heartrending articles that told the 2-7 CAV story for the press during our struggle in Fallujah. Mr. McAllester has held many journalist positons, some include being the Editor for *Newsweek Europe*; he was a former correspondent/bureau chief reporter for *Newsday*, a contributing editor at *Details* magazine, an Adjunct/Visiting Professor for the City of New York Graduate School of Journalism, Senior Editor for *Time Magazine*, and *Time Magazine* Europe Editor.[105]

In his many years as a correspondent, Mr. McAllester covered numerous conflicts in addition to Iraq, such as Kosovo, Israel, the Palestinian Territories, Afghanistan, Turkey, Nigeria, and Lebanon.[106] He has also authored several books, some of which are *Beyond the Mountains of the Damned: The War inside Kosovo*, *Blinded by the Sunlight: Emerging from the Prison of Saddam's Iraq*, *Bittersweet: Lessons from my Mother's Kitchen*, and *Eating Mud Crabs in Kandahar: Stories of War and Food by the World's Leading Correspondents*.[107]

I am very grateful to Mr. McAllester for his work in documenting what we did in Fallujah. I know I struggle with putting into words what happened back in November of 2004, or any deployment for that matter. Key passages from the stories he wrote about 2-7 CAV really illustrate the personal nature of the battle. He has a captivating style in his delivery of our story that is the perfect complement to my raw and unpolished military version of events. Many Soldiers do not always feel like sharing the details of their combat experiences, but thanks to Matt, members of 2-7 CAV do not have to; he was our voice.

---

105 Matthew McAllester, "Linkedin Profile," LinkedIn.
106 Ibid.
107 Ibid.

Now that we have laid out the origins, history, and personalities so crucial to this story, it is time to enter the lion's den of the City of Mosques...

6. SPEARHEAD

We spend tears now that we may conserve blood later. Polynikes was not seeking to hurt you tonight. He was trying to teach that discipline of mind which will block out fear when the trumpets sound and the battle pipers mark the beat. Remember what I told you about the house with many rooms. There are rooms we must not enter. Anger. Fear. Any passion which leads the mind toward that "possession" which undoes men in war. Habit will be your champion. When you train the mind to think one way and one way only, when you refuse to allow it to think in another, that will produce great strength in battle…Habit is a mighty ally, my young friend. The habit of fear and anger, or the habit of self-composure and courage.[108]

—Steven Pressfield, *Gates of Fire*

SEPTEMBER 2004 – SUNDAY (AM) 7 NOV 2004

After Najaf, 2-7 CAV quietly returned to normal operations in and around Taji. There was a feeling as early as September though, that there would be a big operation to deal with Fallujah sooner rather than later. I knew before I moved up to Taji to join 2-7 CAV at the end of September that Fallujah was a persistant topic of reporting and debate. I followed

---

108 Pressfield, 139.

it closely through all the intelligence channels and figured it was only a matter of time before the Marines tried to pacify the city again. The question I and everyone else in 2-7 CAV had was, "Will it be like Najaf? Will it be an all Marine affair like April? Will they ask the Army to help out?"

Those questions were finally answered in October when we were granted DIRLAUTH (Direct Liaison Auhtorized-the ability to talk diretly to the Marines without having to go up the Army chain of command for approval) with the 1MARDIV. I know as a staff, however, we had all been leaning pretty far forward in the foxhole and doing some mission analysis on our own even without the official word. A good staff led by insightful leaders acts on intuition and we did. 1st Lt. Erwin used his night shift, which provided him lots of time for intelligence preparataion; basically studying and researching the enemy in Fallujah. It was always a favored topic of discussion when I would come into the battalion headquarters in the mornings.

The humble leader that Lt. Col. Rainey was would lead him to tell you that we were selected once again for this operation because we were the path of least resistance.[109] Our mission was one of an economy of force (as mentioned before) and it was easier to cut us loose than one of the more decisively engaged battalions down in Baghdad. While this is true, I also don't think that the past experiences of the battalion with the Marines hurt either. Were we requested by name? Not quite I don't think, but maybe pretty close? Who knows?

According to Maj. Gen. Richard F. Natonski, 1MARDIV (ground combat element of the 1MEF) he went to his boss Lt. Gen. Sattler (1 MEF Commander) and requested Army mechanized forces.[110] He did not want a protracted fight like April and he wanted Army units to penetrate quickly and disrupt enemy command and control ahead of

---

109 Rainey, 2006, 111.
110 Richard F. Natonski, interview by Laurence Lessard, April 5, 2007, 5.

clearing Marine battalions.[111] Lt. Gen. Sattler had a couple units in mind that had assisted the MEF in August, so he told Lt. Gen. Thomas Metz (Multi-National Corps-Iraq CDR) and Gen. George Casey (MNF-I) that "we need some Army units and it would be really great if it happened to be these two particular battalions."[112] Their reply was simply, "Okay, you got them."[113] One of those two battalions Lt. Gen. Sattler was referring to was 2-7 CAV. If it all actually happened that way, only a few people really know, however, it does make a Soldier feel really good about what they are doing to think that even for a second a unit the caliber of the 1st Marine Division "Guadalcanal" wanted you by name. Exhiliration doesn't quite describe the feeling.

That feeling only lasted for a short while. We all knew (the staff) that it didn't mean anything to be asked to help if we didn't come through in "the crunch." There was no resting on our laurels. This honor brought with it a lot of work and preparation. Lt. Col. Rainey, leading by example as always, immediately went to school studying the plans and operations of his peers in Baghdad, Lt. Col. Gary Volesky (2-5 CAV), Lt. Col. Miles Miyamasu (1-5 CAV) and Lt. Col. Tom MacDonald (1-9 CAV).[114] The staff all followed his lead, guided along the way by Majs. Karcher and Jackson "pinging" the Marines for as much information as possible to help us prepare.

Shortly after being notified of DIRLAUTH we sent a planning cooridation team by Blackhawk helicopter from Taji to Camp Fallujah towards the end of October. Maj. Karcher took a few of the staff to get in on the grassroots level of the planning. I vividly remember meeting Col. Shupp that night with Maj. Karcher and the rest of our party and instantly knowing that working for this man was going to be a pleasure and that there was no way I wanted to let him down. He had one of the

---

111 Ibid., 6.
112 Ibid.
113 Ibid.
114 Rainey, 2006, 111.

single most compelling and magnetic personlities I had ever encountered. Before we broke down into smaller planning groups, we started out in a big conference room. Not too long into the meeting we had a rocket attack and the building shook and dust dropped down from the ceiling. After a quick check to make sure everyone was okay, we shook the dust off, and drove on. This was the first sign of many to come that this was going to be a good partnership. Focused, unfazed, and straight to the business at hand, rockets or no rockets.

Later that night, we broke down into our individual functions of responsibility. I was swept away by the Fires guys and the Mike Battery/4-14 FA Commander. After getting an overview of their current operations (mainly counter rocket and mortar fire), we moved to a narrow side room full of computers and maps and I was briefed on their conceptual fire support plan. Marines are very good at fires integration into the maneuver fight, especially when it comes to close air support (CAS). I was not disappointed in what I heard. Quite simply, I was blown away. At my disposal would be my own organic 120mm mortars, one dedicated battery of 155mm howitzer cannons (M198s, "God's Gun" from M/4-14), Marine and Army rotary wing aircraft (Cobras and Apaches), and Navy, Marine, and Air Force fixed wing aircraft (Hornets, Strike Eagles, and AC-130 Spectre Gunships) stacked from 9,000-30,000 feet.

After taking all this in, I wondered how I was ever going to be able to plan and integrate all this in just a short period. After a night of being overloaded with planning and learning about the Marines' system of controlling indirect and aircraft assets, I went to breakfast early with the Mike Battery Commander. I was starving. I noticed while I was in the chow hall, unlike in an Army dining facility, there was not a single weapon on the ground under a chair while anyone ate. All weapons were still slung across their chests or in their lap. It was such a simple habit and action characteristic of true warriors to maintain their personal weapons at the highest levels of readiness that says so much. This was the second sign in my mind our two units were very similar and would work well together. My initial impressions from this whirlwind night were on my mind the whole way back to Taji. I knew I had a lot of work to do and I could use some help.

Lt. Col. Rainey demonstrated his foresight in requesting from the 1st Cavalry Division that we be given an Air Liaison Officer (ALO) and team of Joint Terminal Attack Controllers (JTACs) to help manage the aircraft that would be available to us for the fight. He also asked for a lawyer to help interpret the rules of engagement (ROE) to make sure we were always in compliance. This was the help I had been hoping for and I did not even need to ask; it is like he read my mind. Capt. Gentile and his Toxin Team showed up about a week before we left at the end of October/beginning of November for Camp Fallujah to arrange for the arrival of the entire battalion and begin the final stages of planning for the assault on Fallujah.

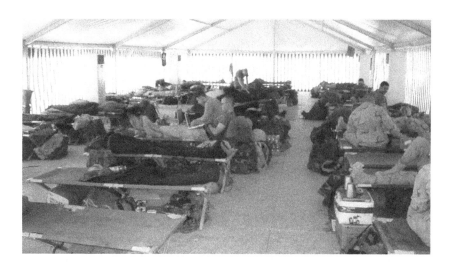

Accommodations at Camp Fallujah
Source: Photo courtesy of Mike Erwin

We were well received once again by the Marines when we met up at Camp Fallujah. The First Team was taking care of getting us all the best equipment and personnel for the fight (i.e., JTACs and a lawyer) and the Marines spared no expense in housing us as comfortably as possible. They set up a "tent city" for the battalion, complete with living quarters, a motor pool for our vehicles, and shower and mess facilities. Capt. Morris saw to it that all our guys had to do was roll in, park, and unpack. Maj. Karcher, Capt. Gray, and I continued to work and refine details of the assault. The battalion road marched down from Taji, leaving on or about 3 November.

When Lt. Col. Rainey arrived, we had to iron out one of the biggest details in the plan: how to penetrate into the city on a wider front.[115] RCT-1 was already the main effort for the 1MARDIV and our battalion was to be the main effort for RCT-1. We were going to be the main effort of the main effort! It was an exceptional honor and an extraordinary responsibility.

Lt. Col. Rainey and Maj. Karcher felt very strongly that if our penetration was on a wider front it would be more effective and make the best use of our mechanized force, especially as we were the leading and initial force into the city.[116] Originally, our axis was solely down Phase Line (PL) Henry, which would only allow roughly two tanks to be in the fight at one time and the battalion had 14 tanks and 30 Bradleys to employ.[117] A lot was riding on how well we accomplished our mission. The first proposal offered (to increase our battlespace) to Col. Shupp was denied, as he did not want to increase the RCT's sector by adding more territory.[118] RCT-1 was initially responsible for one quarter of the city with RCT-7 responsible for the other three quarters. At the time, the intelligence preparation of the battlefield told us that the RCT-1 sector for the assault into the Jolan, was the enemy's strongpoint. The forces there were their center of gravity and this was the spot they would make

---

115 Ibid., 113.
116 Ibid., 113-14.
117 Ibid., 113.
118 Ibid., 113-14.

their last stand. Adding more territorial responsibility could take away from the mission of destroying the enemy in this pivotal area of Fallujah. This neighborhood was characterized by old Byzantine architecture, illogically arrayed narrow streets, and buildings very close together. This was very tough terrain for mechanized and armored forces to fight in and engage the enemy.

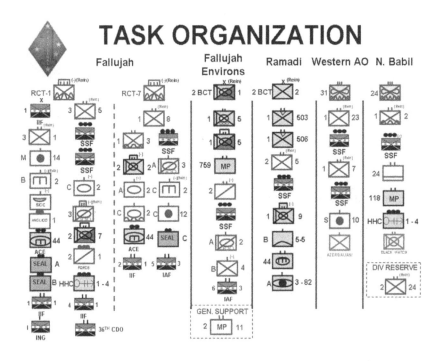

TASK ORGANIZATION

Source: Matthews, Matt. *Operation Al Fajr: A Study in Army and Marine Corps Joint Operations.* Fort Leavenworth, KS: Combat Studies Institute, 2006.

Lt. Col. Rainey went back to the drawing board with Maj. Karcher and came up with another alternative. Their second proposal had A/2-7 CAV as our battalion main effort conducting a frontal assault on three axes wide enough to get our firepower into the fight to destroy enemy forces, disrupt command and control, and seize the Jolan Park (the park was assessed as critical key terrain that supported the enemy's internal lines of communication and supplies; this was the center of the center).[119] We offered to have Apache Company lead the way instead of 3rd Battalion, 1st Marine Regiment (3-1 Marines). C/3-8 CAV, Cougar Company, would still attack along its initial axis of advance, securing the flank of A/2-7 CAV with the ability to conduct spoiling attacks from east to west in the event Apache needed any assistance.[120] We would then conduct a passage of lines with 3-1 Marines and let them continue on with their clearance of the sector.

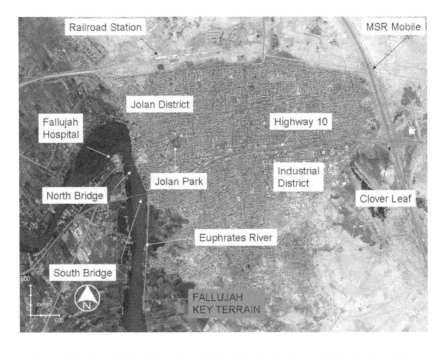

Source: Matthews, Matt. *Operation Al Fajr: A Study in Army and Marine Corps Joint Operations.* Fort Leavenworth, KS: Combat Studies Institute, 2006.

The logic and intuition of Lt. Col. Rainey and Maj. Karcher was that

---

119 Ibid., 114.
120 Ibid.

in an urban environment everything was a frontal assault. Even though it was not the optimal form of manuever, by trying to do some sort of sexy manuever, it would have just opened up a lot of flanks for attack and complicated the plan.[121] Lt. Col. Rainey described this exchange of suggestions and concerns by saying,

> *It wasn't a negotiation. Colonel* Shupp denied my first request and granted my second request. He listened to feedback and made a decision...The fact that he was receptive to listening and ac-knowledging the fact that we probably were the experts on how to employ mechanized assets impressed me....[122]

Lt. Col. Rainey and the rest of us were not the only ones that were impressed with their counterparts for this bold undertaking in Fallujah. Col. Shupp in referencing the planning for the battle remarked,

> *The whole time, Karcher and* 2-7 are working like they had been with us all the time. I can't stress enough to you that these guys were incredible, with everything from their languague to their morale to their attitude, just fit in perfectly with the Marine Reg-iment...Very aggressive, very good officers, knew their craft and were prepared to go into combat and do the right thing.[123]

This period of time, as you can imagine, was extremely busy. So much to do in so little time. We still had to finalize the battalion operations order (OPORD), rehearsals to execute, and maintenance to conduct. The tactical operations center (TOC) at Camp Fallujah was packed (stand-ing room only) for the order given by Lt. Col. Rainey. It actually didn't last as long as one might think for an operation of this scope and scale.

---

121 Ibid., 119.
122 Ibid., 114.
123 Shupp, 2006, 53.

The fact that we were "[w]orking from a battle plan weeks in the making" as described by embed reporter Matt McAllester, the staff, other than a few modifications, had most of the work done, the commanders already knew their mission, their task and purpose, which allowed them to do much of their troop leading procedures concurrently. [124] They had even given their initial mission back briefs prior to leaving Taji and adjusted on the fly as we received more information once we were on the ground at Camp Fallujah.

Lt. Col. Rainey made sure that the plan was covered in detail one more time during the final OPORD brief and drove home again the mission and purpose. He reminded the battalion leadership:

> *[y]ou're rested, you're ready, and* we're prepared...This is going to be the biggest fight any of us will do in the near future. No matter what we think about the Iraqi war or the Iraqi government, this fight is 100 percent about terrorists, terrorists who want to come to your home and kill you. It's going to be a tougher fight than Najaf.[125]

He knew as long as the leaders in that tent had that information, they would know how to execute to accomplish the mission with or without him or one of the more senior officers. There were a few questions at the conclusion, then everyone split off to brief their own subordinates, ensuring that same mission and purpose were understood at the lowest levels, the level where this battle would be won.

I attended my first combined arms rehearasl for the mission in Fallujah. It was conducted inside a large auditorium on Camp Fallujah with everyone sitting in tiered seats except the big wigs (generals, regimental/battalion commanders and key higher echelon staff). I was with Stroker talking through our fires and air support plan. Capt. Glass recalls that Col. Shupp and Lt. Col. Rainey were doing all the speaking for RCT-1

---

124 McAllester, "Long-planned attack begins," A04.
125 Ibid.

and 2-7 CAV, so he sat towards the back with the other company commanders and went over and over in his head what he was supposed to
do.[126] During the rehearsal, Capt. Chris Brooke found the CAS plan to
be very impressive, which showed fixed-wing air assets "stacked upon
each other for what seemed like miles."[127] There was a buzz, electricity,
and feeling in the air that what was about to take place was larger than
we could comprehend at the time. So many indicators, like the inordi-
nate amount of aircraft diverted to support this mission, was just unheard of before. Capt. Brooke, C/2-7 CAV recalled there was, "So much
energy at all levels: the individual level, the organizational level, both the
leaders and the Soldiers."[128]

I thought of this period as the calm before the storm. This time was
wearisome because it contained such a broad range of emotions from ex-
hilartion and excitement on one end, to varying levels of fear and anxiety
on the other. All these differing emotions were visual to the acute observer watching us in our tents on Camp Fallujah even though most of
"the men [had] seen major action before, unlike many in Iraq."[129] Matt
McAllester noticed the tension building among the battlion as,

> [e]ach night, soldiers have lain in big blue-and-white tents in a
> camp outside Fallujah on dark khaki cots, watching DVDs on
> their laptops, chuckling in the private oblivion of headphones.
> Others have sat in corners with a pack of cards, a voice rising
> with a win, others groaning. Somewhere nearby, an artillery bat-
> tery has for days been booming irregularly but often, targeting
> Fallujah and making even some of these experienced soldiers
> leap. "You need new underwear, you just let me know," they like
> to call out to each other when they spot each other flinching. Sol-

---

126 Glass, 2006, 73.
127 Brooke, 2006, 269.
128 Ibid.
129 McAllester, "Long-planned attack begins," A04.

diers have not been coming to Chaplain Jonathan Fowler with jokes. They have been coming to him "to get good with God," he said. These are young men, some 19 years old, and they know that they might not come back from this fight.[130]

The thing was everyone was preparing themselves in their own way for the looming fight. Mr. McAllester recounted a revealing conversation with Staff Sgt. Carlos Santillana, 24, of Abilene, Texas.

> *"Everyone's different," he said. He* gestured to his friend, Sgt. Akram Abdelwahab, 28, from Spartanburg, S.C., "He's listening to music and getting psyched up," Santillana said, as Abdelwahab smiled. "I just like to sleep. If you don't think about dying, if you don't try to come to terms with it," Santillana said, "there's something wrong with you.
>
> "If you're ready and at peace with wherever you're going to go, you're good to go," he said. "If you ain't afraid of dying, you got issues....Whenever you come close to it, you find God real quick."[131]

This theme continued in another conversation inside our tents where Mr. McAllester realized,

> *[r]eligion and faith pops up* in conversation with just about every soldier with the 2nd Battalion. "I do a lot of praying," said Staff Sgt. Michael Clifford, 39, of Arlington, Texas. "Making sure He's taking care of us up there. The way I look at it, we're not over here to kill. We're here to separate good from evil." As an observant Catholic, he can't bear the idea of Iraqi civilians dying in this fight. "That was my first thought is I sure hope those civilian people get out of there," he said. "I pray for the innocent. The in-

---

130 Ibid.
131 Ibid.

surgents will come into their homes and take away their homes. What can they do?"

During those last few days before the battle, the calm was disturbed by a rocket attack that hit near our TOC and killed a Soldier (not from our unit, but another supporting the operation). This was a timely reminder of the gravity of the situation we were in and which still faced us. Comanche Company, led by Chris Brooke, dealt with the calm and company nerves by maintaining their equipment and rehearsing. He explained,

You make sure every single piece of equipment that's coming through the breach works like it's supposed to. Then you check it again. You rehearse everything. You rehearse your actions as an organization, and in your quiet time you rehearse your own actions in different situations.[132]

Just like everyone else, I had to spend time trying to calm my mind and emotions. I watched movies, listened to music, slept, but was most thankful we had Chaplain Jonathan Fowler, our battalion chaplain, with us. He had a small but much appreiciated church service one morning near a concrete bunker before we left Camp Fallujah. It was a bright and sunny day, fitting for receiving the good Word. I was ready for whatever lay ahead of me, but I had one burning question that weighed heavily on my mind. I spoke to Chaplain Fowler about this after the service. I asked him if I died in Fallujah would I know my wife and son (we only had one child at the time; we are blessed with four amazing children now) in heaven and would we have the same relationship in heaven as on earth? The answer: God doesn't reveal those details, only that heaven is the perfect place. It wasn't the answer I was looking for, but the Chaplain reminded me that you have to have faith in the Lord that all will be as He

132 Brooke, 2006, 269.

intended. I thought about those questions a lot and even more after our reconnaissance by force and my first contact with the enemy in Fallujah.

1st Lt. Jimmy Campbell, our Scout Platoon Leader, who had been out north of the city scouting routes to our Task Force Support Area (TFSA) all that day before led myself, Capts. Glass and Twaddell, their first sections for the assault into the city, and one of my FSOs, 1st Lt. Matt Fox, on a reconnaissance by force to the northern edge of the city under cover of darkness. Stroker and I travelled in one of the scout humvees. We took cover amongst a small cluster of farm buildings near the train station on the northern edge of the city. Capts. Pete Glass and Ed Twaddell wanted to get eyes on the breach site (it was planned to go through the railroad tracks on the western side of the train station and the perimeter berm around Fallujah), the three axes of advance for Apache Company, and a general idea of the Cougar Company axis of advance down PL Henry, which was hidden behind the train station.[133] In the course of our probing reconnaissance, Pete's guys spotted an enemy fighting position on top of a building and engaged and destroyed it with a main tank round from about 1,500m.[134]

Stroker and I used the recon as an opportunity to validate our communcations with the RCT for coordinating air strikes. Communication was good, however, we weren't able to get any aircraft for missions during the reconnaissance as they were all being utilized by higher headquarters at the time for shaping operations over the city. Instead, I instructed Matt to get his hands a bit dirty and call for some 155mm fire missions between the breach site and the city to corroborate reports that the peripheral area of the city was heavily covered with improvised explosive devices (IEDs). We didn't spot any secondary explosions, indicting that the area was mined, but it was a great opportunity for my newest FSO to get in on the action and possibly quell a few nerves, myself included.

---

133 Rainey, 2006, 117.
134 Ibid.

1st Lt. Fox (left) and Staff Sgt. Mercado (right) sporting some trophies in Fallujah
Source: Photo courtesy of Eric Hough

He was a very good young officer and I was quite impressed with his performance. He had a seasoned and quality Fire Support NCO in Staff Sergeant (Staff Sgt.) Julian Mercado that I had worked with for many years as well, that would take good care of him in the upcoming operation. Returning to Camp Fallujah, I continually ran through my mind how I was going to manage my portion of the fight from my Bradley Fighting Vehicle (BFV), I didn't want to wait anymore. I wanted to get into the city and get the battle started. The wait was pain-stakingly agonizing.

SUNDAY (PM) 7 NOVEMBER – 8 NOVEMBER

Finally, the waiting was over on the evening of 7 November. That night we left Camp Fallujah for our TFSA and assault positions while the enemy was preoccupied with the assault of 3rd Light Armored Reconnaissance (LAR) Battalion and the 36th Commando (CDO) of the Iraqi Special Operations Forces (see map below). They attacked up the peninsula to seize the Fallujah General Hospital and the far side of the old (north) and new (south) bridges across the Euphrates. It was extremely congested and confusing getting off the camp, but like any traffic jam, once the lead elements got moving and everyone was spread out, everything worked out smoothly. Good work by our scouts and 1st Lt. Campbell really helped us out, as we were able to roll right into our positions. We slowly made our way above the city and then worked our way in from north to south. I pulled in with my Bradley to the abandoned plaster factory right after daybreak and I was one of the last elements of the battalion to leave Camp Fallujah.

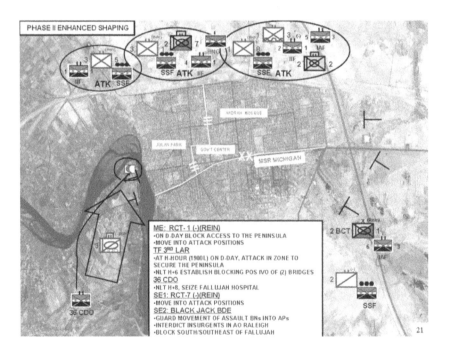

Source: Matthews, Matt. *Operation Al Fajr: A Study in Army and Marine Corps Joint Operations.* Fort Leavenworth, KS: Combat Studies Institute, 2006.

At that point, like a well-oiled machine, everyone in the headquarters set to work getting the TOC operational. That evening we would be crossing the line of departure and there would be no looking back. It was time to get ready. This was the time when I found out I would not be accompanying Lt. Col. Rainey and Maj. Karcher into the city. Stroker and I would be controlling fires and air support from the TOC. I was not ready for this truly devastating blow. I had always been told that the proper place for a fire support officer was at the side of the commander, ensuring responsive fires and CAS to support based upon their guidance. I did not understand Lt. Col. Rainey's decision, but I would shortly.

2-7 Tactical Operations Center (TOC) nestled in the plaster factory
Source: Photo courtesy of Lee Gentile Jr.

2-7 Tactical Operations Center (TOC) under the Fallujah sunset

Our homemade and old school latrines. *Source:* Photos courtesy of Mike Erwin

During the afternoon on Monday, 8 November, 3rd Battalion, 5th Marines (3-5 Marines) attacked, seized and occupied the apartment complex just to the northwest of Fallujah. The complex was to be used as a command post for the battalion, as well as Col. Shupp and the RCT headquarters. At 1900, Col. Shupp ordered 3-1 Marines with a company of Iraqi National Guard (ING) to seize the train station.[135] After the assault force eliminated the defenders, they could use the train station as a position to provide cover for Marine engineers to breach the railroad tracks and open the mine/IED-field between there and the city. The breach took a lot longer than expected to conduct and mark due "to the normal fog and friction of combat" in the words of Lt. Col. Rainey.[136] Frustrated by the delay, our forces waited around six hours or so in a cold miserable rain, knowing that each passing hour was another hour of darkness that we would not be able to take advantage of to fight the enemy in limited visibility.

Capt. Chaos waiting in the cold November rain. *Source:* Photo courtesy of Eric Hough

---

135 Shupp, 2006, 56.
136 Rainey, 2006, 119.

During the wait, Maj. Karcher described watching "this death and destruction rain down on the city, from AC-130s [Air Force fire support aircraft] to any kind of fast-moving aircraft, 155mm howitzers, you name it, and everybody was getting in on the mix."[137] In some respects, this was the first way that the breach delay actually benefited our efforts. As Lt. Col. Rainey saw it,

> ...*we had a lot of* tough fighting in the city, we had won the fight by the time we crossed the line of departure based on how effective two things were. First, there was the unmanned aerial vehicle (UAV) collection...The second thing was that we had two AC-130s committed to this the night before the fight.[138]

These were two of the assets bringing "the rain" that Maj. Karcher observed. The delay in the breach allowed them more time to shape the battlefield on our behalf. Lt. Col. Rainey felt "[t]he decisive point, where we started winning and the enemy started losing, was right about the time we LD'd [crossed the line of departure] because the enemy was reeling."[139]

9 NOVEMBER

Early on the morning of 9 November at approximately 0130, the battalion began to move through the breach just to the west of the train station and into the city.[140] The Marine engineers brought up a mine clearing line charge to detonate any mines or IEDs south of the berm down to PL April (the perimeter road on the northern edge of town—see map

---

137 Karcher, 2006, 202.
138 Rainey, 2006, 117.
139 Ibid., 118.
140 Karcher, 2006, 202.

below). The berm was opened with 2,000-pound Marine aircraft bombs and D9 bulldozers.[141] Marine engineers then blew the train tracks apart with TNT and moved the pieces out of the way. The last step left to open the door into the city and begin the fight in earnest was to plow and proof the lane. Matt McAllester observed that 2-7 CAV, "pushed through clouds of desert dust toward the front row of houses in the northwestern corner of the insurgent-held city. Drawing fire from rebel positions, they let loose with their guns in what was intended as an overwhelming attack."[142]

C/3-8 CAV had the privilege to be the first unit of the RCT-1 main effort to throw themselves into the battle for Fallujah. Cougar Company was led by their 1st Platoon Leader, 1st Lt. Omari Thompson, who plowed the breach, pushing any remaining mines or IEDs out of the way while another tank proofed it with their roller.[143] Lt. Col. Rainey reminisced as the battalion was completing the breach that there was a time as a younger officer at the National Training Center doing breaches that he thought to himself, "When the hell are we ever going to do this shit?"[144] Well, there he was with his battalion conducting a breach to get into one of the biggest battles of our generation. I guess that is as good a time as any!

Staff Sgt. Reyes completed rolling the lane and then drove his roller straight into a building on the far side of PL April to leave as a visual marker; then one of the crew dismounted the tank in contact with the enemy, disconnected the roller allowing it to drop from the front of the tank.[145] It proved to be quite a good visual marker too, identifying the end of the breach lane for the rest of the forces passing through the breach in the dark.

---

141 Shupp, 2006, 55-56.
142 McAllester, "Driving toward the heart of enemy," A07.
143 Glass, 2006, 73.
144 Rainey, 2006, 116.
145 Ibid.

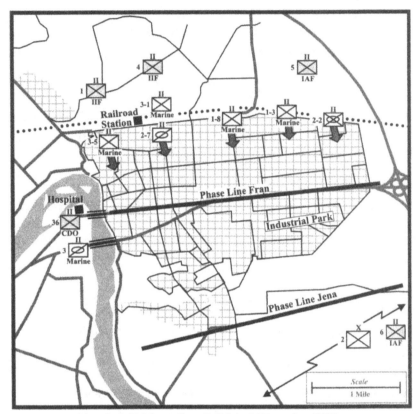

Map 4. Initial Assualt on Fallujah, 9 November 2004.

Source: Gott, Kendall D. and John McCool, *Eyewitness to War: The US Army in Oper-*
ation Al Fajr, an Oral History. Fort Leavenworth, KS: Combat Studies Institute Press,
2006.

With the enemy occupied by 3rd LAR's task force on the peninsula
and preparation fires softening up targets in advance of the battalion, the
enemy's center of defense was exposed as 2-7 CAV rumbled on line to
attack in force. *Newsday* reporter, Matt McAllester described the scene,

> *By 2 a.m. here a* column of heavily armored Abrams tanks and
> Bradley Fighting Vehicles entered Fallujah along the perimeter

roads and down some of the main arteries toward the heart of the city. The vehicles crawled past palm trees swaying in the wind and apparently deserted two-story homes, many of them behind walls and metal gates. Viewed on an infrared screen inside one of the Bradleys, an Abrams tank swiveled its main gun to the east and fired repeatedly at suspected insurgents who were firing Kalashnikov rifles at the Americans.[146]

Capt. Chaos led his two platoons of tanks and one platoon of mechanized infantry due east along PL April. He turned south on PL Henry and positioned his company to destroy the enemy to his front and protect the flank of Apache Company and his partner Capt. Ed Twaddell. The company attacked with two tanks abreast up front with two Bradleys in behind, ready to engage over the top of the two lead tanks.[147]

Capt. Ed Twaddell's Apache Company with two mechanized infantry platoons and one tank platoon was right on their heels and quickly spun themselves south from PL April into their three-pronged axis of attack and began to push into the heart of the Jolan in order to seize and hold the Jolan Park (Objective-OBJ Pennsylvania). Capt. Chris Brooke and his Comanche Company after having to be ground guided through a Marine unit that was blocking the breach made it down PL April and set up a series of attack by fire positions south from the intersection of PL April and PL Henry, securing the battalion's line of communication (LOC) back to the TFSA.[148]

Lt. Col. Rainey, with Command Sgt. Maj. Mace in the back of his Bradley and his wingman, Maj. Karcher, followed in behind Cougar Company. This position allowed them the ability to bound east and west between the two lead elements. Maj. Karcher, at this time, was responsible for the maneuver of the battalion, Maj. Jackson was in the TOC coordinating

---

146 McAllester, "Driving toward the heart of enemy," A07.
147 Rainey, 2006, 120.
148 Brooke, 2006, 270.

staff support, and Lt. Col. Rainey was managing the synchronization of both aspects of the fight. From Lt. Col. Rainey's perspective based upon his experiences as a junior leader, it could sometimes take a lot of time and energy to get people going during maneuver training, however, this was not the case in Fallujah. The times had changed in his opinion because,

> *[i]n the absence of guidance,* these great Soldiers are going to act. They want to make contact with the enemy. They want to do their job and, quite frankly, within the ROE, they want to kill everybody they can kill. The challenge as a commander is harnessing that energy and that violence of action — because they're going to go somewhere…It's not about getting them to go; it's about getting them to go where you want…[149]

Winning battles requires awareness of more than just what is going on in one sector. The commander has responsibility for seeing the bigger picture and knowing where everyone is on the battlefield to ensure everyone is working towards the same objectives. This awareness is extremely important when employing indirect (artillery) fires and close air support. In order for Majs. Jackson and Karcher to "be able to do their job, my job as commander was to make sure we knew where everybody was and that we were controlling that violence," stated Lt. Col. Rainey.[150] Ghost 6 described the energy and violence of action he was referring to with an analogy from a former company commander of his who envisioned,

> *fighting in an urban environment* was like playing tackle football in a hallway. Then you throw tanks and Bradleys in there and it's like a demolition derby in a hallway…You're the guy behind the main effort company or in between companies, and you listen to

---

149 Rainey, 2006, 131.
150 Ibid.

the radios, leverage your digital systems, and you pay attention to who's really where and make sure you're doing the right thing.[151]

It did not take long for the chaos of battle to become apparent. The enemy was ready to fight against whoever showed up. It did not matter what uniform they wore, what vehicles they drove, or what weapons they carried. According to Command Sgt. Maj. Mace, the enemy was "brave in their own right, but they were just amateurs fighting professionals—and the professionals had the better toys."[152] The city was littered with debris and obstacles in an attempt to slow down the assault. The Muj' (term used by the Marines for the enemy made up of former regime elements, terrorists, and criminals) employed tactics whereby they attacked in 2-3 man groups with small arms fire, RPGs (rocket propelled grenades), IEDs, and mines. It seemed like every single building had sandbags in the windows and was a prepared fighting position. Small arms, of course, do very little to armored forces, however, RPGs, IEDs and mines can cause serious damage.

The insurgents quickly realized that hit and run attacks could increase their longevity and getting close to armored vehicles made armament systems and sights less effective. The enemy tried to target the rear of vehicles and early on one Muj' made such an attempt. He avoided detection by the Ghost 6 Bradley crew (too close to show clear in their optics), but was creamed by Maj. Karcher's gunner according to Command Sgt. Maj. Mace while lining up an RPG shot on the back of his Bradley.[153] 1st Lt. Michael Duran, from A/2-7 CAV, had to engage and destroy a 3-man RPG team so close to one of his platoon's Bradleys because the crew inside just saw a blur in the sights and could not fire upon the enemy themselves.[154] The insurgents were getting within 10 feet of some of

151 Ibid.
152 Mace, 2006, 188.
153 Ibid., 187.
154 John Urrutia, interview by Matt Matthews, March 14, 2006, 214.

the vehicles. They might have had more success if vehicle commanders were not so effective in looking out for each other and their wingmen.

The battalion was making steady contact across the whole front against attacking Muj', IEDs, and potential vehicle-borne improvised explosive devices (VBIEDs), but kept up a deliberate and methodical push to the Jolan Park. The guidance from Lt. Col. Rainey was to keep moving and to make room for 3-1 Marines behind us, but not to leave an enemy element of a squad or larger size for the Marines to fight if possible. As the 9 November morning wore on, Apache Company was closing in on OBJ Pennsylvania (the Jolan Park) and began taking their first indirect fire of the battle. Resistance was stiffening as they approached this key piece of terrain and 2nd Platoon, with Sergeant First Class (Sgt. 1st Class) John Urrutia, was about to be right in the middle of it.

C/3-8 arrayed along PL Henry pushing south securing the flank
Source: Photo courtesy of Eric Hough

Capt. Twaddell's plan called for a mounted assault through the park first, then to dismount and clear back through the park on foot from south to north. Apache 6 wanted his dismounts to catch the enemy while they were still stunned by the initial mounted attack. The park was an open area, actually an amusement park with rides, including a Ferris wheel. Once dismounted, Sgt. 1st Class Urrutia, and his platoon had the task of clearing and securing a section of the park. Two Marine engineers [a Lance Corporal and a Pfc. with about 20 pounds of C4 explosives] accompanied them.[155] Once on the ground, the reference point for their direction of movement and their clearing operation was a water tower and some multi-story buildings that overlooked the park. As they made their way to the objective, the Marine engineers came in handy, as there were walls 10-15 feet high that had not been visible during the map recon of the objective that needed breaching.[156] The squad used the C4 to blow holes in the walls to work their way through the park towards the building complex, instead of scaling them and risk undue exposure to enemy fire.

The platoon began to clear the building complex as loud speakers across the street from the park blared in Arabic a warning that Americans were coming to root out any insurgents that had stuck around to fight.[157] 1st Lt. Duran and a squad over watched an adjacent building, while Sgt. 1st Class Urrutia cleared a building with another squad, which included Staff Sgt. Nathan Scott, Corporal (Cpl.) Willie Hudgens, and Specialist (Spc.) Lucas Bondo.[158] They entered a two-story building with Hudgens on point moving left with Bondo and two others moving right.[159] A Muj' fighter was discovered hidden underneath a table with a weapon ready to ambush the team, but Spc. Bondo quickly engaged and killed the insurgent with several well-aimed bursts from his Squad Automatic Weapon.[160]

---

155 Ibid.
156 Ibid., 215.
157 Ibid., 216.
158 Ibid.
159 Ibid.
160 Ibid.

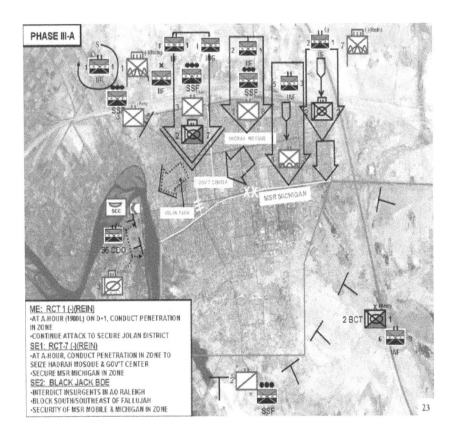

Source: Matthews, Matt. *Operation Al Fajr: A Study in Army and Marine Corps Joint Operations.* Fort Leavenworth, KS: Combat Studies Institute, 2006.

The pressure felt by the insurgents from attacks on three sides: 3rd LAR on the peninsula to the west, 3-5 Marines in the northwest, and 3-1 Marines working their way south from PL April left no major forces to guard the critical piece of terrain of the Jolan Park. 2-7 CAV was able to successfully penetrate the defensive belts of the enemy and land themselves deep in the rear of the insurgents. The seizure of the Jolan Park was a devastating blow to the enemy. A/2-7 CAV uncovered an extensive weapons cache and VBIED factory that would no longer be available for the Muj' to use.

1st Lt. Duran and Staff Sgt. Scott in Fallujah
Source: Matthews, Matt. *Operation Al Fajr: A Study in Army and Marine Corps Joint Operations.* Fort Leavenworth, KS: Combat Studies Institute, 2006.

In all, more than 500 mortar rounds were discovered, 30-40 130 and 155mm artillery shells, mortar tubes, around five surface-to-air missiles, grenades, RPGs, and about 300 pounds of TNT or PE4 (plastic explosive).[161] The VBIED factory had one fuel tanker assembled with three 155mm artillery rounds in the tank, a black BMW with the doors lined with C4 and five 155mm artillery rounds wired and ready for use, and one blue BMW all wired, but no ordnance hooked up yet.[162] With Jolan Park secure, it was time to pass 3-1 Marines through our lines and let them continue their attack deep into the heart of the byzantine structures of the Jolan itself. Matt McAllester captured the 3-1 Marine battalion entry into Fallujah.

A crescent moon appeared between the gray clouds that hung over Fallujah…and from across the fields came the sound of music. It was the "Ride of the Valkyries," by Richard Wagner, booming from the loudspeakers of a Humvee. The music used in a famous scene in the 1979 movie "Apocalypse Now" echoed over the rooftops of the northern edge of this now war-torn city. Apache helicopters circled, firing Hellfire missiles through the fresh light of morning. A black flag fluttered in the breeze, the flag of the militant group now calling itself al-Qaida in Iraq. Its leader is the Jordanian-born militant Abu Musab al-Zarqawi and the American military is hoping he's holed up inside the Jolan neighborhood in northwest Fallujah, the area of the city now under concentrated attack. Troop-laden vehicles from the 3rd Battalion 1st Marines streamed across the desert into the city along a route made safe only hours earlier by the Abrams tanks and Bradley Fighting Vehicles of the Army's 2nd Battalion of the 7th Cavalry Regiment.[163]

Another positive outcome of the breach taking so long was we were able to conduct the passage of lines in the daylight, which really helped,

---

161 Ibid., 216-17.
162 Ibid.
163 Matthew McAllester, "A lot of fighting to do still," *Newsday*, November 10, 2004, A02.

as it was already a very complicated task, which there had not been time to rehearse beforehand. The passage of 3-1 Marines was complete after about four hours, at which point Apache and Cougar consolidated their positions to the south/southeast to prevent enemy reinforcements moving into the Jolan from behind or on the Marines' flank and waited for follow-on orders.[164] The insurgents could not have been happy with losing such key terrain in the Jolan Park, but they were able to exact a small bit of revenge with a 127mm rocket attack that evening. The Voice recounted the afternoon.

All around, all the time, explosions—large and small—broke the silence. There was the insistent pounding of the Bradley 25-mm cannons, the whizz of the insurgent rocket-propelled grenades, the crack of incoming sniper fire and the wall-shaking boom of the Abrams tank cannons…The men [A/2-7] lay prone on the floor of the cinderblock building, sleeping for the few moments they could grab, oblivious to the explosions outside. Alongside one wall lay an Iraqi man, a piece of cloth draped over his face, shot dead by the platoon as they approached the building early in the morning…Strewn on the ground were leaflets advertising the $25-million price on Zarqawi's head, air-dropped over the past months in Fallujah. At 5:10 p.m.… a massive blast hit the building we were working in. Fire erupted outside the room's window, and we were thrown to the ground. Dust filled the entire building, so thick that it was impossible to see. Soldiers shouted out for one another by name through the whiteness. "Anyone hit?" called out Staff Sgt. Carlos Santillana, who was in the next room. As the dust cleared a little, a 2-foot-wide hole in the roof became visible, and a rocket emerged from the gloom, embedded

---

164 Rainey, 2006, 122.

in the floor 10 feet from our work area. Soldiers watched quietly, looking at one another, looking away, looking at the wounded.[165]

We had several casualties due to that attack and lost one of our sniper teams and our Marine ANGLICO (Marine Air and Naval Gunfire Liaison Company) team due to wounds, some pretty serious.[166] The battalion was having early success. Lt. Col. Rainey discussed his assessment of the battle to date with Matt McAllester after recharging his batteries living by one of his maxims, "Sleep is a weapon."[167]

It's going well. Initially it was light. Kind of like I expected. They stay down at night. They know we can see them well, he said. I don't think his strategy is doctrinal defense, urban defense, Rainey said, smiling at the thought of his enemy. I think they're committed fighters who want to die fighting.…There's a lot of fighting to do still.[168]

The battalion had been moving so quickly there was no need to stop our momentum. We achieved our first 24-hour objective in only 12-hours; therefore, Lt. Col. Rainey continued to push the attack onto the next objective. That night and into the early morning on 10 November, C/3-8 CAV maneuvered onto and secured OBJ Virginia (mosque and graveyard) to the south of the Jolan Park (see map below).

---

165 McAllester, "A lot of fighting to do still," A02; "Grim reality, up close," ibid.
166 Rainey, 2006, 121-22.
167 McAllester, "A lot of fighting to do still," A02.
168 A02.

C/3-8 Fire Support Team looking for targets
Source: Photo courtesy of Eric Hough

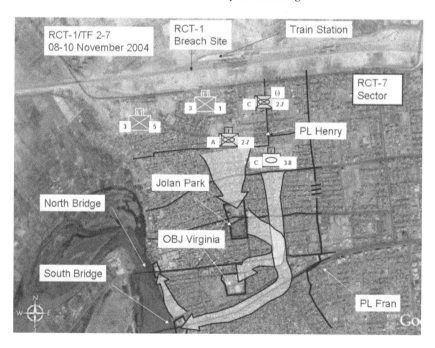

Source: Matthews, Matt. Operation Al Fajr: A Study in Army and Marine Corps Joint
Operations. Fort Leavenworth, KS: Combat Studies Institute, 2006.

10 NOVEMBER

In order to free up C/3-8 CAV to continue the attack south to OBJ Virginia, Lt. Col. Rainey had needed to commit CPT Chris Brooke and Comanche Company solely to keeping PL Henry open and protecting the seam between us and RCT-7 to our east. Comanche Company had been in constant contact throughout the day on 9 November. Just like 3-1 Marines were experiencing further west, many of the enemy after being badly bloodied by the heavy armor of Apache and Cougar had doubled back, holed up, and were waiting for hopefully softer targets. They were now reemerging to face Comanche.

Comanche 6 had his company performing section-sized movements to contact, forcing the resurfacing Muj' to engage his company on their own terms.[169] At this time, all across the battalion's front the enemy seemed more emboldened to attack during the daytime. One night of 2-7 CAV heavy armor decimating them was enough for most of them to go to ground in hours of limited visibility. Capt. Brooke described Comanche's fight to keep the LOCs open.

We experienced heavy contact in the alleys separating Henry and George [the boundary with RCT-7] throughout the first day, and engaged enemy elements both fighting from within fortified buildings and repositioning through the alleyways...we engaged and destroyed all personal vehicles to reduce the VBIED threat to friendly elements, and called for indirect fire on any buildings that appeared to be fortified. Platoons [at night] were ordered to continue to conduct movements to contact, but instead of attempting to maneuver on insurgent positions, they were to fix the enemy with 25 millimeter/coax while the company fire support officer (FSO) [1st Lt. Matt Passarell] and the enlisted tactical

---

169 Brooke, 2006, 270-71.

air controller (ETAC) coordinated for indirect and fixed-wing aviation fires.

The right mixture and proper application of combined arms combat power at the lowest levels by young leaders like Staff Sgts. Young and Lewis, and Sergeant (Sgt.) Loukus of Comanche Company, were completely denying the insurgents the ability to use the RCT seam (the boundary just east of PL Henry between RCT-1 and RCT-7).[170] This prevented their ability to reinforce across the boundary and wreak any havoc on the Marines clearing house to house in the Jolan from the rear, as well as, keeping the ever more critical LOC open back north. Comanche cleared all the buildings along the route, not letting the insurgents rest and keeping them on guard constantly.

Around 48 hours into the battle, casualties started to mount. 2-7 CAV had a few from the attack on the Jolan Park, but 3-1 Marines, who were clearing behind the battalion already, had 20-30 killed in action and many more wounded.[171] The battalion offered our tracked medical evacuation (MEDEVAC) vehicles to the Marines to use. Col. Shupp said they were a "godsend on the battlefield," removing their casualties to the rear right up PL Henry and out of the city.[172] Capt. Chris Brooke and his company keeping PL Henry open was literally a lifeline for many Soldiers and Marines. Their efforts on PL Henry were saving lives and severely disrupting the enemy's ability to mount an effectual attack on the rear and flank of friendly forces.

From around 2300 on 9 November moving into the early morning hours of 10 November, C/3-8 CAV began its attack to seize OBJ Virginia. This objective was more commonly referred to as Martyr's Cemetery (a big open area just to the south of the Jolan Park, see map above). Lt. Col. Rainey knew there was risk involved as Cougar moved south. They

---

170 Ibid., 271.
171 Shupp, 2006, 59.
172 Ibid.

would expose both flanks as they maneuvered ahead of all elements of both RCT-1 and 7.[173] Their turn on PL Fran exposed their left flank to the southern section of the city, which had been undisturbed to this point. Once they had control of the objective, however, it had the potential to be a very advantageous position.

Drawing on experience from Najaf in August, the battalion knew that open urban terrain like Martyr's Cemetery was a typical rallying point from which the Muj' would wish to conduct their mobile defense, similar to the Jolan Park.[174] This fact ensured Martyr's Cemetery would be a place worth them defending, providing great opportunities for us to engage the enemy. Once it was within our possession, the open space also offered great fields of fire for our longer-range weapons systems. We knew since it was an important location, the insurgents would try to take it back, and their counterattacks would offer further chances for killing insurgents. In an interview by Matt McAllester, Lt. Col. Rainey described the effects the continuous pressure was having on the enemy.

> ...*the Army and Marine units* that have pushed into and around Fallujah have dispersed the insurgents from suspected strongholds. While an ideal situation would have been to cordon most of the insurgents in the northwestern Jolan neighborhood, Rainey said, dispersion has pluses. "I think it's good because they're off balance and disorganized," he said, standing in his command tent just outside the city last night. The scattered teams of insurgents call for frequent movement and vigilance in all directions..." The biggest variables are probably the all-around aspect of the fight...the 360-degree fight when the enemy can come in from behind, to your sides and from above," said Maj. Tim Karcher, the chief strategist for this heavily armored battalion. ...They have a home team advantage, the commanders said. But that is the

---

173 Rainey, 2006, 122-23.
174 Ibid.

only advantage. The U.S. troops can fire from several points and hit the same target, Karcher said. If the enemy is "in the second story of a building in different rooms, I can engage from different directions," he said. Within minutes, U.S. commanders can call in artillery, air, or mortar strikes. They can send tanks or Bradleys, which are almost impregnable to most insurgent weapons. And they can use snipers and overwhelming numbers of highly trained soldiers.[175]

Capt. Chaos used the same method as Capt. Twaddell with the Jolan Park to seize OBJ Virginia. He assaulted through the objective first, then dismounted and cleared. Sure enough, as soon as the company started clearing the objective they started receiving fire, but not from just anywhere. Cougar Company was taking heavy fire from the mosque in a corner of the cemetery. The mosque was also most likely a huge enemy weapons cache, command and control node, and heavily fortified fighting position. The level of fortification of the mosque required Lt. Col. Rainey and Maj. Karcher to request extra help for Cougar Company. They coordinated with Attack 6, the commander of 1-227 Attack Aviation Battalion, who we worked with on a daily basis in Taji.[176] After about 30 minutes, Cougar was advised to take cover and an Apache launched two Hellfire missiles into the strong point. After additional bombardment by artillery and mortar fire, Capt. Chaos sent in his infantry and finished off the rest of the insurgents, either killing or capturing those that were still alive. Though we were accomplishing our mission ahead of schedule, we were not rushing the fight. If anything, we were taking more time, but our effectiveness was allowing us to reach our objectives sooner than we had planned.

Today's counterinsurgent tactics require a different rulebook from the sort used during last year's invasion [2003], when the United

---

175 Matthew McAllester, "Urban War Strategy," *Newsday*, November 11, 2004, A03.
176 Rainey, 2006, 124.

States took control of the entire country in three weeks. This assault on a single city of 250,000 may take almost as long. Engaging regular armies on the battlefield is much easier, commanders say, than fighting guerrillas in narrow alleyways and on rooftops. "The mantra in the U.S. Army is slow is fast because you've got to go slow to go fast," Karcher said. "Urban combat demands more time." Each house, each block, will be searched as the soldiers and Marines hunt down the people who sometimes seem invisible, commanders said…."There's no reason to rush," said Marine Col. Mike Shupp, commander of Regimental Combat Team 1. "Today [we're] closing in and will clean out the Jolan neighborhood. It will be an infantry attack, house by house primarily…a steady steamroller coming down the road at them." Shupp, like many commanders, has for years studied urban and counterinsurgent tactics, reading up on the American war in Vietnam, British experience in Iraq and elsewhere, French anti-guerrilla tactics in Algeria. "We're being guided by all these principles," he said.[177]

Lt. Col. Rainey updated Col. Shupp as to the battalion's status and situation, offering to continue the momentum by moving onto our next objectives, Kentucky and Ohio (the eastern bridgeheads of the old and new Euphrates River bridges, see maps above) and Inchon 6 responded to continue the attack.[178] The battalion liked that decision, and liked it a lot! We had the momentum, the enemy was reeling, why not continue to press the advantage. Cougar Company consolidated on OBJ Virginia and screened the southern flank of the RCT. Apache Company refitted and topped off with fuel at the TFSA after handing over the Jolan Park to the Marines and came roaring back south to get back into the fight.

Lt. Col. Rainey wanted Ed to conduct two platoon-sized attacks—one each on OBJ Ohio, then Kentucky (north to south). Capt.

---

177 McAllester, "Urban War Strategy," A03.
178 Rainey, 2006, 124.

Twaddell, however, came back up on the net, said that he understood, but after studying the situation, he preferred to move below OBJ Virginia and attack from south to north, hitting Kentucky first then Ohio, for several reasons.[179] First, he did not want to attack between two units (3-1 Marines and his friend Capt. Pete Glass's Cougars). Second and more importantly, he reasoned that so far, all our attacks had been from north to south and he thought by attacking south to north this time he would surprise the enemy and gain a marked advantage over them on two strong targets.[180] Lt. Col. Rainey recognized,

> *Captain Twaddell had done everything* I'd asked of him to do and he did a great job down in Najaf. And you know, the ability to acknowledge that one of your guys doing the fight might have a better idea than you is not something that's lost on me, so I told him if that's what he wanted to do, he could do it.[181]

Apache commenced the attack around 0900 on the morning of 10 November. Ed experienced sporadic contact south of OBJ Virginia and as he approached OBJ Kentucky, the enemy defended with approximately two squads.[182] With Ed attacking quickly, and with the luxury of 25mm cannons, he made quick work of the Muj' on the objective. OBJ Ohio was very similar as around 10-15 insurgents tried to make some sort of fervent stand, but only managed to last all of three or four minutes before being destroyed.[183]

Instead of running the risk of a blue on blue incident (fratricide) with 3-1 Marines or 3-5 Marines by staying on the objectives as they worked their way in that direction, Capt. Twaddell pulled his company off both

---

179 Ibid., 125.
180 Ibid.
181 Ibid.
182 Ibid.
183 Ibid.

objectives and maintained over watch on both in case the Muj' got any cra-
zy ideas about trying to retake them. The 2-7 CAV disposition at the time
was Cougar Company on OBJ Virginia, Apache Company over watching
OBJs Kentucky and Ohio, Comanche Company securing the LOC along
PL Henry, and the staff with TOC security elements securing the rear area.
A rear area the enemy was putting to the test. Matt McAllester reported,

> *At 6 p.m. Tuesday [9* November], a rocket-propelled grenade
> landed near the tent [TOC] of the 2nd Battalion commanders
> and everyone rushed for flak jackets and helmets....Insurgents
> were attacking from the rear—not from Fallujah but from the
> farmland of troubled Al Anbar province. Bradleys immediately
> pounded several areas with red and green tracer rounds, plumes
> of dust mushrooming from the desert. Snipers searched for in-
> surgents through telescopic sights. One soldier seemed to have
> grudging respect for the wiles of the insurgents. "They're doing
> what they should do," said Sgt. Matthew McCreery, 24, of Cor-
> vallis, Ore. "They're attacking our logistics." Officers said all the
> camps on the outskirts of the city had been attacked in recent
> hours. Shortly after 10 p.m., another whoosh was followed by
> an explosion—an incoming RPG. In their small way, insurgents
> are bringing the battle to the Americans. Stay still for too long
> in Iraq, whoever you are, and you will almost inevitably get hit. [184]

Consequently, at this time the battalion was 48 hours into combat
and had already seized all original objectives for the whole battle. This
was theoretically supposed to be the end of the Second Battle of Fallujah
(Operation Phantom Fury) for the Ghost Battalion. There was an ominous feeling, however, that this was not all that Fallujah and its defenders
had in store for us. To the south lay half the city still untouched...for now.

---

184 McAllester, "Urban War Strategy," A03.

7. TOXIN

For what can be more noble than to slay oneself? Not literally. Not with a blade in the guts. But to extinguish the selfish self within, that part which looks only to its own preservation, to save its own skin. That, I saw, was the victory you Spartans had gained over yourselves. That was the glue. It was what you had learned and it made me stay, to learn it too.[185]

—Steven Pressfield, *Gates of Fire*

Every moment from my initial arrival at 2-7 CAV in September through the end of the battle in late November was an experience in uncharted territory. All I brought to the table were some preconceived notions about what I was supposed to be doing, some doctrinal knowledge from my Officer Basic Course, and my fire support experience from my time as a tank company fire support officer in Kuwait in 2001-2002. This was going to be O-J-T (on the job training) at its finest. The best part, however, was the fact I had a great group of people in support that would help plan and execute the battalion fire support mission. We became a very tight and cohesive team that, no matter the circumstances, knew failure was not an option and believed we would find a way to accomplish the mission, no matter what.

Our role in support of the maneuver companies was serious business

---

185 Pressfield, 332.

that had a widespread effect on the battle itself. It was conveyed to us that,

[t]here's no doubt about it: you can't win at anything without infantrymen on the ground physically taking it. But the easiest, most effective and least casualty-producing-on-friendly forces way to fight the enemy—even in an urban environment—is with fires.[186]

Toxin TACP with Marine ANGLICO outside Fallujah (Left to right) Capt. Gentile, Senior Airman Joshua Gianni, ANGLICO Marine, Senior Airman Brian Tatum, Staff Sgt. Isaac Ralph, Airman First Class (Airman 1st Class) Gregg McGhee, ANGLICO Marine, ANGLICO Marine, Airman 1st Class Chris Komorek, ANGLICO Marine, Airman 1st Class Kyle Sharp Source: Photo courtesy of Lee Gentile Jr.

Our mission was to make the fight as easy as possible for the infantryman on the ground and save as many of their lives as possible by destroying the enemy first. The name of this super-team was "Toxin." The team consisted of our organic 2-7 FSE (Fires Support Element or HQ), with

---

186 Rainey, 2006, 131.

our three company FISTs (Fire Support Teams), and Toxin from the US Air Force [a HQ team and three tactical air control party (TACP) teams]. The Air Force personnel fit right in with our unit and began bonding immediately. The same went for Capt. Gentile and I as well.

I was so impressed with how well we integrated that I found myself thinking of everyone as Toxin, even my own people. It also better conveyed the image I had in my mind of how I wanted the enemy to feel about our handy work. I wanted to be toxic to the Muj'. Taking nothing away from "2-7 Fire Support Element or FIST", but those were not the identifying titles I saw our team getting excited about and taking pride in. Moreover, Toxin just downright had a nice ring to it when you said it! At the last minute, we also had attached Neutron Tango 25 and 30 (Navy SEALs with apparently no names, at least that we were allowed to know) and a team of Marine ANGLICOs.

2-7 CAV Fire Support Team at Camp Fallujah after the battle (Back row left to right) Sgt. Simien, 1st Lt. Parrot, 1st Lt. Passarell, Spc. Rodriguez, Spc. Mc-Callister, Spc. Garcia, Sgt. 1st Class Howard, Pfc. Gill, Staff Sgt. Montano, Capt. Tyler (Front row left to right) Spc. Manning, Spc. Hough, Staff Sgt. Mercado, Spc. Price, Private (Pvt.) Clark, 1st Lt. Fox, Spc. Creel, Pvt. Bown
Source: Photo courtesy of Coley Tyler

The resources available to our team for this fight were unheard of before in any of our previous collective experiences. In fact, utilizing close air support to begin with was not a mission that the Army trained much at all and there was a lot of dedicated aircraft for Fallujah, hence our Air Force reinforcements. We also had one sole battery of 155mm howitzers in direct support of our RCT (M/4-14), whose commander I had already met, and spent time with building a personal relationship. All indirect fire and air missions in theater were highly regulated by the rules of engagement (ROE). Because ROE can be problematic to apply at times and in certain situations, my team was assigned a lawyer (former artilleryman), specifically for that reason. He was instrumental in keeping my conscience free of any doubt that we took any inappropriate actions.

The plan I came up with was simple. The Marine headquarters made it possible by ensuring every fire supporter, from the frontline all the way back to Camp Fallujah and all aircraft, had the exact same imagery, graphics, and maps. I had nothing to do with this, of course, but these were the base documents that made planning so much simpler. I owe it all to the great work done by the Marines in preparation for the battle. It was no small feat to distribute such a quality product, which had every city block and building labeled and numbered for quick reference. This allowed us to swiftly talk pilots onto targets and call for fires.

Since we were the main effort for the main effort in the early stages of the battle, which meant as soon as we passed through the breach, our fire missions and air requests were the highest priority in the battle. Being the #1 priority gave me goose bumps and a lot of anxiety. Many Soldiers and Marines were counting on me. The adrenaline and excitement of the first three or four days of the battle helped keep me awake as we ran 24-hour operations.

Our 120mm mortars were our close target asset that I pretty much turned over to 1st Lts. Fox, Parrot, and Passarell. I would monitor their requests to the mortar platoon for any issues, but the structured employment of all the assets in the fight, which I will describe later, made that possible from a clearance standpoint. It also made them just a bit more responsive to the company's needs, and there was no one but the enemy to our front.

The 155mm howitzer support requests still came through me at the battalion level and I used them to prosecute targets in advance of our front-line trace and out of danger close range. Capt. Gentile was doing the same thing with our air assets. Stroker and I would fight the deep fight and destroy as much of the enemy as we could before our battalion got there, and then if we missed anything, our mortars would take care of the rest. These were not puny little mortars either. Col. Shupp described our mortar tubes saying,

> *Our 60 and 81 millimeter* mortars are great to go ahead and attack the enemy out in the open and hit him on the rooftops, but our Marines found out that when you take an Army 120-millimeter mortar and drop it on top of a building, it's dropping a floor.[187]

Two very helpful frameworks built and used to fight this battle were concepts developed by the Marines. These were very important in easing the difficulty of directing fires and air sorties during the battle. First was the CFL Box, which was four coordinated fire lines (CFLs) forming a box that allowed surface-to-surface assets to fire into the box without further coordination.[188] Secondly, and most useful, was Keyhole CAS, explained in the below diagram.

---

187 Shupp, 2006, 59.
188 Keil R. Gentry, "RCT-1 Fires in the Battle of Fallujah," *Field Artillery*, November-December 2005, 27.

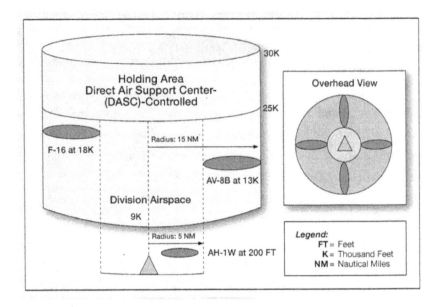

The 1st Marine Division's Keyhole Template for Airspace Control for Operation al Fajr. The template shows the different possibilities for attacking the same target and one way to stack aircraft that are supporting the same target. The forward air controller or joint terminal attack controller (JTAC) work the geometry of the situation to best support the mission, calling in aircraft from their respective holding areas and controlling them as appropriate in the terminal phase of the attack *Source:* Gentry, Keil R. "RCT-1 Fires in the Battle of Fallujah." *Field Artillery*, November-December 2005, 27.

So, going back to our mortars, I knew based upon these concepts (and I told the mortar platoon and my guys this) that as long as our firing solution maximum altitude stayed below where there were any aircraft stacked, and we were not firing through an aircraft stack (dark ovals above) our fires were clear. We were already within the ring of aircraft battle positions also, so the air overhead was always clear from our position north of Fallujah (see map below). The battlefield geometry allowed us to speed up the approval process for engaging targets.

With our TOC being so close to the city, we were able on many occasions to see rotary aircraft engage from right near where we were located. The plan was set, we had conducted our fire support rehearsal, and we were just waiting for "game time."

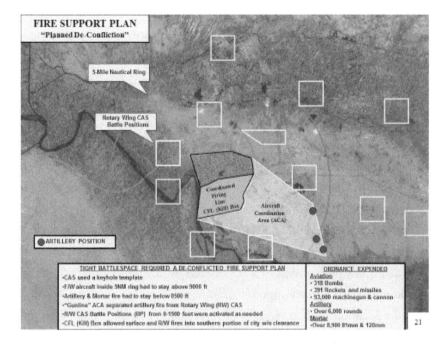

Fallujah Fire Support Plan
Source: Hunt, Maj Todd M. *Operation Al Fajr: The Battle for Fallujah.* 2004.

This was personally one of the more difficult periods for me, going back to Lt. Col. Rainey's decision to keep me at the TOC to execute my fire support plan early on 8 November. Over the past few days and weeks I had spent a lot of time familiarizing myself with my Bradley (Artillery version equipped to function as a fire support vehicle) and rehearsing with my crew. I needed to because my generation of FSOs did not have that piece of equipment. We had the Fires Support Team Vehicle that was integrated with the M113 chassis (Vietnam era), which was very slow and had many mechanical problems along with no real vehicular defense (weaponry).

I did all this because everything I knew about fire support told me that during this battle I would be right on the heels of Lt. Col. Rainey or Maj. Karcher helping support the fight. I did a good job of hiding it (I think), but I was crushed. This was what I had joined the Army to do, the moment and ultimate test of my skills as an artilleryman and Soldier. Everyone like me lived for this chance. I was about to be put into the preverbal biggest game of my life and I was relegated to the bench...so I thought.

What turned out to be the case though was, Lt. Col. Rainey was smarter, more insightful, and had a better understanding of my role in the upcoming fight than I did. I had not made the connection between my plan, the terrain of Fallujah, and how that affected my location during the battle. For Stroker and I to fight the deep fight, I needed to be in a place that I could see what was going on, to be able to engage my targets and manage the chaos the battle created. Being in a Bradley, as part of a quick penetration to seize key terrain in an urban environment, would make that almost impossible. Impossible unless I dismounted and found a location high enough to observe from, at which point I would be disconnected from the units of my battalion as they continued the attack. This would leave me in the middle of the Marines trailing behind us trying to clear the city. I would quickly have become a security problem or just another Bradley 25mm cannon to engage the enemy with without the ability to bring all the other firepower I had at my disposal in support of the fight.

Just as I had never used a Bradley before in my career, I had also never used an unmanned aerial vehicle (UAV) as an observer or used chat on a computer to coordinate for close air support. This was very different from the old ways of just an FM radio, a set of eyes, and a map method of fire support that I grew up with. These tools, however, were at my disposal in the TOC. Whatever feelings of disappointment I still had of not being a part of the assault were soon overtaken by the magnitude of the situation at hand and the myriad of tasks associated with familiarizing myself with these new methods of calling for fire. It was during this period that Capt. Gentile shared with me the tradition and rite of passage of pilots receiving their call signs. Of course, Capt. Gentile's was Stroker and as a testament to our ever-growing relationship, he desired to include me in the tradition as much as he could. He professed that even as a non-pilot he could not keep calling me by a normal name; he just was not used to doing that and therefore declared me "T-Bone" henceforth.

My Kevlar cover from the battle sitting on my Fallujah shelf in my library
Source: Photo courtesy of Coley Tyler.

Funny thing is that call sign has stuck with me to this day. Capt. Gentile's call sign is the product of stereotypical male humor that is even funnier after a six-pack. It is simply Stroke 'r Gentile...which some may say is childish, but what guys aren't at some point in time. As for my call-sign, the 'T' is for Tyler and the Bone is still a bit of a mystery. Either it just came to Stroker in a moment of clarity in battle or it could have been a friendly chide on the country life of my youth where cow tipping was still a practiced form of entertainment, we may never know.

Our fires area was located in the short leg of our 'L' shaped TOC (see picture in Chapter 4), which was nestled into the dusty opening at the base of an abandoned plaster factory. The battle captains, Capts. Conley and Chapman, were next to us to our right and the intelligence section on the far side beyond with Capt. Gray and 1st Lt. Erwin. The meeting area and communications were in the back long leg. We were all close enough to communicate without getting up, but enough space to have room to work without feeling like sardines. 1st Lt. Erwin, soon after the TOC was up and running, got our Raven UAV flying into the city and connected those feeds along with other feeds to the Marine UAV platforms so we could get "eyes on" or observe inside Fallujah.

Mike, as the intelligence, surveillance, and reconnaissance (ISR) officer, provided very close to real time intelligence, saving lives by determining enemy locations before we arrived.[189] He and I worked very closely in Fallujah. He was one set of eyes for me to use. Stroker with his equipment, to include chat ability to the air cell at the RCT, was also able to receive live video feeds from aircraft. This allowed us to use them as recon assets, in addition to engaging targets we had found. These were another set of my eyes. Sitting in assault positions not too far away were six teams of fire and air support specialists. They were my last set of eyes. Those were the eyes that would be going into the lion's den of Fallujah itself.

A few hundred feet away in another building in the factory complex was the ALOC with Capts. Morris and Brown, as well as 1st Lt. St. Laurent. Protecting our TFSA was 2nd Platoon, Bravo Company, 2-162 Infantry (2/B/2-162 IN) from the Oregon National Guard [Platoon Leader (PL) Chris Kent and Platoon Sergeant (PSG) Pete Salerno].

---

189 Erwin, 2006, 51.

They were instrumental in providing our security while our focus was in the city. We appeared to be an easy target and took quite a few mortar/rocket attacks and an actual probing attack (described by Matt McAllester in the previous chapter) by a few insurgents over the next week or so before 2/B/2-162 IN and our scouts neutralized the threat.

Over the next few pages is a mission summary of some of the key air engagements of Team Toxin. Unfortunately, we did not keep such accurate records for the artillery or mortar missions fired. They were just too numerous. I do know that our mortars contributed significantly to the over 8,900 mortar rounds fired and that our artillery requests were a large portion of the over 6,000 155mm rounds fired into Fallujah in those couple of weeks in November.[190] The mortar Platoon Sergeant, Sgt. 1st Class Glenn Greanya, commented that he had never shot that many rounds in his entire career up to that point and many of those rounds were in support of our Marine brothers. Whenever our tubes were free and they needed them, they got them. They already had the radio frequency and they just called them up and shot them as if they were their own. That is about as joint as operations can get. Stroker recorded the following mission summary of our contribution to the air campaign during the Second Battle of Fallujah.

TOXIN 40 TEAM FALLUJAH MISSION SUMMARY[191]

Written and compiled by Lieutenant Colonel (Lt Col)* Lee G. Gentile Jr., USAF

---

190 Maj Todd M. Hunt, "Operation Al Fajr: The Battle for Fallujah," (2004), 21.
191 Lee Gentile Jr., April 3, 2012.

*Stroker was a Lt. Col. at the time he compiled his notes from the battle into electronic form.

MISSION OBJECTIVE

Provide Close Air Support to the 2nd Battalion of the 7th Cavalry Regiment (2-7 Cav) during OPERATION PHANTOM FURY, the invasion of Fallujah, Iraq.

MISSION SUMMARY

NOTE: Local time is all times Z (Zulu) + 3 hours. Example 1600Z is 1900 local time.

Around 1600Z on 7 Nov 04, the 2-7 Cav began moving to the vicinity of the Train Station in preparation for movement through the breach into Fallujah. Toxin 41 and 43 were imbedded with Cougar and Apache Companies, respectively, as the 2-7 main effort. Toxin 42 was assigned to Comanche Company, the battalion reserve, protecting the major LOCs in and out of Fallujah. Toxin 40 was located with the 2-7 TOC, at Objective Otter, coordinating between the teams in the field and higher headquarters.

At 2130Z (8 NOV), Toxin 40 engaged two barriers on PL Henry with Hellfires from Tycoon 15 (2 x AH-1-Cobra helicopters) setting in motion the 2-7 Cav attack. Toxin 40 used Basher 75 (AC-130 gunship) to recce Apache and Cougar's ingress, while Tycoon 15 covered their flanks and Comanche's ingress.

During the ingress, Basher 75 identified personnel with weapons patrolling the roof and guards at the entrances of a building on the East side of PL Henry between PL Elizabeth and Fran. Toxin 40 directed Basher 75 to engage the building, enemy personnel, and vehicles at 2220Z, noting secondary explosions from the building and one of the vehicles.

Matt McAllester wrote of the early fight for Fallujah for readers around the globe that,

"American and Iraqi forces attacked the insurgent-held city of Fallujah last night…As an AC-130 gunship targeted suspected car bombs in the town, and artillery pounded suspected rebel positions…U.S. and Iraqi troops had begun pushing forward into the city after a barrage of artillery scattered burning shrapnel above the heads of insurgents in frontline positions, looking like orange firework bursts and scattering almost certain death on anyone below. The sky above Fallujah filled with enormous explosions and red flares scythed across the desert night as they slammed into insurgent positions. Missiles from an AC-130 gunship patrolling the route of the advancing Abrams and Bradley vehicles shattered cars suspected of being driven by suicide bombers.[192]

Missions continued to support the attack as our lead elements worked their way south to the Jolan Park. We continued to prepare the battle space in advance of our units with our longer-range systems.

Around 0010Z on 9 NOV 04 (which is actually 0310 9 NOV 04), the 2-7 Cav received RPG and sniper fire from a building two blocks to the west of the intersection of PL Henry and Elizabeth. Toxin 40 directed Profane 55 (2 x F-18-Hornet fighter jets) to drop a GBU-38 [Guided Bomb Unit] on the building, resulting in a miss. With the 2-7 Cav still taking fire from that building, Toxin 40 cleared Basher 75 to engage the target at 0033Z, allowing the 2-7 to break contact and continue their move to Jolan Park.

At 0740Z, 2-7 Cav began taking RPG fire from a building east of the intersection of Elizabeth and Henry. At 0807Z, Toxin 40 cleared Profane 33 (2 x F-18) to engage the building with a GBU-12.

On the morning of 9 NOV, as they were obtaining optimal observation positions for themselves and Neutron Tango (NT) 25, Toxin 43 came under heavy small arms and sniper fire. While in their defensive

---

192 McAllester, "Long-planned attack begins," A04; "Driving toward the heart of enemy," A07.

positions, completely pinned down by the intensity of the enemy volley, Toxin 43 and the security element with them were hit by an enemy mortar. Without hesitation, Toxin 43 began assessing and treating an Army sniper and the Marine ANGLICO, who had received the most extensive injuries. Once the injured were stabilized, Toxin 43 aided in coordinating a CASEVAC [Casualty Evacuation] for the wounded despite the continual incoming enemy fire. After the situation stabilized, Toxin 43 and Neutron Tango 25 moved into position and prepared to direct air strikes in defense of their company.[193]

Remarkably, as I am following the reports of the attack in Jolan Park, I flashed back to a conversation I had the night before with the Marine ANGLICO officer that was just wounded. He was not thrilled with his attachment to an Army battalion, it was not a feeling against us personally, but he really wanted to be with his fellow Marines. I could totally empathize with him on that. He was itching for a fight. I advised him to be patient and wait until the battalion had seized some ground first. This would allow him to set up in a secure location so he had a good vantage point for observation. He told me thanks, but no thanks, and that he was leaving right then with his team to join Apache Company. By the time he made it to Ed Twaddell's company they were in a secure location, but the enemy got to him anyway. Within 12 hours, I saw him being MEDEVAC'd* out, severely wounded in the groin area, and his team was out of the fight.

Once the CASEVAC* was complete, Toxin 43, NT 25, and a Navy SEAL sniper team moved to a new OP. Having received several shots from a sniper at their last location, the SEAL sniper team began their counter-sniper operation. In addition to providing CAS to Apache Company, Toxin 43 used their See Spot to aid in the anti-sniper search effort and prepared to use CAS to prosecute the target once identified.

---

193 Gentile Jr.

*Note: MEDEVAC and CASEVAC often used synonymously.

In a pre-coordinated strike on Martyr's Cemetery at sometime early on 10 NOV, Toxin 40 used Hellfires from two Apaches to engage several insurgents firing at US troops from the Mosque in the Northeast corner of the cemetery. The strike suppressed the enemy gunners, allowing Cougar Company to secure the area quickly, with no casualties.

Once Jolan Park and Martyr's Cemetery were under 2-7 Cav control, Toxin 41, 42 and 43 dismounted and secured observation positions to aid in the acquisition and prosecution of targets. Overnight, enemy resistance was light. HUMINT [Human Intelligence] reports indicated an increased VBIED threat and headquarters directed all units to find and destroy unoccupied vehicles in their respective AO [area of operations]. Over the course of the next 72 Hours, Toxin 40 used ISR, AC-130, and fixed wing assets to identify and destroy 16 vehicles with secondary explosions observed from nine.[194]

A typical scenario of UAV and artillery collaboration during the battle involved 1st Lt. Erwin watching the most current live feed from the UAV in our sector and calling me over when he noticed potential targets. Matt McAllester commented on one such occasion,

In the command tent of the 2nd Battalion, Rainey and intelligence officers watched a computer screen that displayed a live feed from an unmanned drone aircraft flying over the city with powerful cameras and positioning systems. From the tent, the officers could see four insurgents firing mortars—the white flash showing up in the backyard of a house—and then moving quickly through the streets. Two of the men appeared to be carrying weapons, probably Kalashnikov rifles. It is this kind of technology that allowed precision targeting from the American forces that sent clouds of smoke erupting throughout the city. From a few dozen yards away, the 2nd Battalion's mortar team fired into the sky—a

194 Ibid.

loud bang followed by the whizz of the projectile heading toward the city in an arc. Several seconds later, loud booms echoed back across the desert to this forward base.[195]

During one of the first days of the battle, 1st Lt. Erwin called me over for what we observed was approximately 15 insurgents with weapons moving through the streets ahead of Apache and Cougar Companies from one fighting position to another. The UAV followed them for a few minutes until they all moved into a building a short distance down a side street off the main attack route. These were the opportunities I was looking for and instantly sprang into action. In about two leaps, I was on my radio sending my call for fire into the Regiment that sounded something like this:

Inchon this is Ghost, adjust fire, over.
Ghost this is Inchon, adjust fire, out.
Grid XX0123456789, over.
Grid XX0123456789, out.
15 enemy in fortified building, HE/PD* converged sheaf in effect, over.
15 enemy in fortified building, HE/PD converged sheaf in effect, out.
Ghost this is Inchon, message to observer to follow.
N, 12 rounds, target AA1234, over.
N, 12 rounds, target AA1234, out.
Direction 1650, over.
Direction 1650, out.

I sprang back over to the screen and a few moments later the adjusting round lands smack dab in the middle of the house. I scream to my

---

195 McAllester, "Driving toward the heart of enemy," A07.

*Note: High Explosive/Point Detonating (HE/PD)

guys, "Fire for effect, fire for effect!" One of them picks up the radio hand mic and calls back:

Inchon this Ghost, fire for effect, target AA1234, over.
Ghost this is Inchon, fire for effect, target AA1234, out.

Seconds later two rounds per tube, 12 rounds total, smash into the position with those 15 Muj' inside. When the smoke cleared, the house was demolished and there were no signs of life from the building or anyone trying to escape the rubble. I call up Inchon after observing the target shortly and confirm with them that the target was destroyed and 15 enemy KIA. In cases where the enemy was on a rooftop or they were escaping from a previously reduced building, I would engage the enemy again, but with ICM (improved conventional munitions). Those rounds had a variable time fuze that caused the round to explode into hundreds of small pieces approximately 10-20 feet off the ground, very similar to a shotgun blast of buckshot, but much, much bigger.

At 1400Z, the 2-7 Cav began taking heavy fire (small arms and RPG) from a building north of the intersection of PL Fran and Henry. Toxin 40 had Rattler 51 (2 x F-18) deliver a GBU-12 on the building, ending the TIC (troops in contact). While on patrol, Comanche Company started taking fire from a building near Henry Field. Toxin 42 identified the building and cleared Rattler 51 to place a GBU-12 on the building at 1435Z. Shortly thereafter, Comanche began taking RPG and small arms fire from another building. Within minutes, Toxin 42 had Comanche mark the target with tracer fire aiding Rattler 51's acquisition of the target, and delivered two GBU-12s to break contact (first GBU-12 was a no guide/dud).

One hour later, the 2-7 Cav began taking small arms and RPG fire from the intersection of PL Henry and Fran. Toxin 40 used Dime 31 (2 x F-18) to prosecute a target on the northeast corner with a GBU-12 and another target on the southwest corner with two GBU-38s, ending the TIC at 1536Z and clearing 2-7's route. Overnight, the 2-7 Cav saw sporadic action in the AO with several TICs. All the Toxin teams identified valid targets while under fire, but were unable to use with CAS because the 2-7 Cav was not the priority effort. Instead, the Toxin teams worked in conjunction with their company FSO to prosecute the targets using imbedded mortars.

Early on the morning of 10 Nov, Toxin 43 was taking sniper fire from an industrial complex at the intersection of PL Jacob and Grace. Toxin 43 worked in conjunction with Neutron Tango 30 and Cougar 14 (company FSO) to put Mortars on the target and end the TIC. Around 1200Z, Comanche began taking fire from the building near Henry Field that was hit the night before. Toxin 42 swiftly engaged the target with a GBU-12 from Profane 51, quelling the TIC and destroying the building.[196]

Troops in Contact (TIC) situations were an opportunity for a little friendly inter-service rivalry competition between Stroker and I. Of course, these are very serious situations, but since it was impossible for one person to get two different assets to prosecute a target at the same time, we tried to see which asset would be the quickest, most responsive, and clear the ROE first—either close air support or artillery fires. Stroker, the pilot, worked the air request, and I as the Red Leg (historical slang terminology for an artilleryman), worked the artillery call for fire. It seemed to us that higher always approved close air support first. Most importantly, however, there was never a request for support that we were not able to assist with fires in some capacity. Sometimes higher did not approve our requests in as timely a manner as we would have liked though. Matt McAllester recalls one of our least responsive moments.

...there was excitement in the command tent of the 2nd Battalion of the 7th Regiment, which is located on the site of a decrepit

---

196 Gentile Jr.

plaster factory on the northern outskirts of the city. The spotters who sit gazing at a laptop screen 24 hours a day had seen a group of about 40 men, some with weapons, collecting in a building... The jets were now almost within range. The heavy artillery guns had the coordinates. More than a dozen men craned for a view of the screen, across tables covered in maps and secure telephones, waiting for the silent eruption of smoke that would mean there were a whole lot less. Nothing happened. "Are they dropping it or not?" asked the battalion's commander, Lt. Col. Jim Rainey, to no one in particular. Another soldier sat at another laptop typing messages back and forth in a secure chat room with a Marine targeter, who was most closely coordinating the strike. "He said, 'Red tape. I'll explain later,'" the soldier said to the crowd, without taking his eyes off his screen. The crowd grew impatient. Everyone had jobs to do. "Damn it," said Maj. Scott Jackson, the battalion's executive officer, walking away. Sometime later, the red tape was cleared. Simultaneously, jets that had flown from aircraft carriers in the Persian Gulf or perhaps a base in Turkey released their guided bombs while ground-based artillery guns unleashed huge shells into the blue sky. The house on the screen disappeared in a massive cloud of smoke. From the rubble, a handful of men staggered out and ran away into nearby houses. That just allowed the spotters to see where they had moved on to. "The rats are trying to scurry about," said Maj. Tim Karcher, operations officer for the 2nd Battalion. Later in the morning, the same system delivered a similar blow to a house where about 15 men had hidden. After that blast, about 10 men rushed from a house next door.[197]

197 Matthew McAllester, "Pockets of resistance," *Newsday*, November 15, 2004, A04.

2-7 Mortar Platoon in action
Source: Photo courtesy of Mike Erwin.

Our lawyer was always right beside us for every mission and would say something like, "Yes, this falls within the ROE, you can do this," or "You might want to wait, see how things unfold before you do it," either confirming or denying the actions we were thinking about taking on every mission. Even following the strict ROE, a lawyer with oversight of our mission calls, and several levels of higher headquarters for approval, our team was not immune from accusations of foul play, however. Below, Stroker recounts our narrow brush with a charge of committing war crimes while in Fallujah.

In October 2004, I deployed from my A-10 squadron, the 74th Fighter Squadron also known as the World Famous Flying Tigers, as a battalion air liaison officer assigned to the 2nd Brigade of the 10th Mountain Division in Baghdad. I had been a Flying Tiger for almost a year, however, I had arrived at our home station while my squadron was deployed to Operation IRAQI FREEDOM, so this was my first deployment. By late 2004, the political situation in Iraq was very fragile and the insurgency was nearing its peak. In order to prevent fueling the growing hatred toward the US presence, all of the ALOs (Air Liaison Officers, including battalion level), and JTACS (Joint terminal attack controllers) had been consolidated at the 1st Cavalry Division Headquarters under the 9th Air Support Operations Squadron in order to provide strict oversight of all kinetic attacks and eliminate collateral damage incidents. My duties at the Division Operations Center included coordination of airlift and ISR (intelligence, surveillance, and reconnaissance), which play a vital role in counter-insurgency operations, and the occasional response to a Troops in Contact call. However, the day-to-day operations in the Division Headquarters were different than what I had trained for and how I envisioned I would be contributing to the war, which left me questioning why I was there.

I had only been in country three weeks when I received orders to forward deploy to Camp Taji to support the 2nd Battalion of the 7th Cavalry Regiment, commonly known as the 2-7 Cav or "Gary Owen", during the upcoming operation in Fallujah. Since this was my first time in combat, I was excited and nervous about the future battle. My TACP (Tactical Air Control Party) teams and I arrived a week prior to the start of the operation and began getting up to speed on the enemy situation, the operational plan, the battalion's scheme of maneuver, and the air support plan. Additionally, we started living with and working with our assigned units; my team and I would be with the battalion's headquarters unit and each of the three remaining TACP teams would be assigned to one of the company commanders. This allowed us to get to know the soldiers we would be fighting alongside of and since we were outsiders, to earn their respect as quickly as possible.

It was 8 November 2004, the opening night of PHANTOM FURY. My ROMADs (radio maintainer, operator, and driver) and I had been at the 2-7 Cav Tactical Operations Center monitoring the radio nets and waiting to respond to requests for air support. It had been six hours since the battalion had commenced the attack on the train station on the north side of the city and the fight was going well. The train station was tactically significant because it threatened the security of the battalion's supply lines for the remainder of the operation and therefore needed to be neutralized. With that objective secure, the battalion began pushing into the north side of the city. In accordance with the pre-attack briefing, we targeted some barriers and observation posts with 500-pound laser-guided bombs in order to clear the lead company's avenue of approach. Additionally, we reconnoitered the primary and secondary attack routes and the surrounding streets for ambush sites and troop concentrations.

The fighting continued into the night when the AC-130s started checking in. Since the 2-7 was the lead unit, an AC-130 was dedicated to our battalion. The AC-130 is an amazing platform, especially during nighttime, close-quarters urban conflict, and I was going to use it to gain every advantage possible for the 2-7. As we directed the AC-130 to methodically sweep the area, we found a large building a block to the east of the primary attack route with personnel patrolling the roof of the building and the perimeter of the compound. As I coordinated the strike, I was filled with emotions ranging from nervous excitement to fear to sympathy to no feelings at all (something I had not anticipated). Although, I had directed the strikes against the barriers and the suspected observation posts, those strikes felt like the attacks I had controlled against the old tanks and fake buildings on the training range at Fort Bragg. However, this was different. This was the first time I would direct an air strike against a known enemy position, I could not physically see the target, and I did not want to make a mistake. After discussing the situation with Lieutenant Colonel Rainey, the 2-7 Cav Commander, and the battalion staff judge advocate, it was determined that this was a legal target in accordance with the ROE (Rules of Engagement) and I began the coordination process with the Regiment and Division to prosecute the target. After receiving higher headquarters approval to employ,

I cleared the AC-130 to fire 105mm delayed-fuse rounds into the building and use 30mm high explosive incendiary rounds to neutralize the personnel. Within a matter of few minutes, the strike was complete and the enemy was denied a tactical position from which they could have easily attacked our battalion as we pressed into the city.

My teams and I continued to control air until November 12th when the Marines took control of the city. By the time the fighting was over, the 2-7 CAV TACP teams, which consisted of four two-man JTAC teams, a five-man ANGLICO (Air and Naval Gunfire Liaison Company) team, and two Navy SEAL JTACs, were credited with the destruction of 15 fighting positions, 14 observation positions, 10 rocket powered grenade teams, 4 command posts, 3 sniper teams, 2 weapons caches, a mortar team, 16 vehicles, and 300 enemy KIA. By all accounts, we believed we had served honorably, achieved our objectives, and accomplished our mission until I received a phone call on 17 November.

I had just left the morning BUB (Battalion Commander Update Brief), when my ROMAD said "Sir, Colonel X called for you and asked that you call him immediately." I told my ROMAD thanks, walked over to the Fire Support Officer's M-113 where my workstation was set up and called the Colonel.

"Sir, this is Captain Gentile. You asked that I call you ASAP."
"Were you Thud One Zero on 8 November?"
"Yes Sir, I was."
"Did you control an AC-130 attack on a building on 8 November?"
"Yes Sir, I did."
"Captain Gentile, you are under investigation for war crimes under article 3 of the Geneva Convention for attacking a hospital, you have the right to remain silent…"

I was devastated. As the Colonel read me my rights over the phone and explained that, I would be contacted about this matter later, I starting recalling all the events of that night. Although the phone call had lasted only a matter of minutes, it felt like an eternity as I recounted the details of attack and started questioning my decision for that night.

Was it a valid target?

Did I follow the ROE?

I coordinated with higher headquarters, right?

What did I miss?

Because of several days of only getting 2-3 hours of sleep, my memories were not as sharp as I needed them to be. Luckily, I had taken detailed notes and had several witnesses to help me recount the events accurately. After 30 minutes of frantically gathering my defense, I went to talk to Lieutenant Colonel Rainey. I told Lieutenant Colonel Rainey about the phone call and the target in question, and as I started to present my case he stopped me and said, "Lee, it was a valid target in accordance with the ROE. I approved that target. I gave you the clearance to drop. I'm responsible, not you! You and your boys did an amazing job. Because of you, the 2-7 Cav didn't lose a single soldier to enemy action. Don't worry about the charges. I'll take care of them!"

To date, this is the single greatest act of leadership I have ever witnessed. Lieutenant Colonel Rainey did not know anything about me and since I was not assigned to the 2-7 Cav, only attached for the duration of the operation, he did not have to provide me any top cover...yet he did! I never heard back from that Colonel who called and read me my rights, and it wasn't until months later that I heard the other half of the story. The investigation had started when a video claiming that US forces had attacked a hospital on the first night of the operation showed up at a Middle East News outlet. The video showed "patients" lying in their beds with gunshot wounds to their heads and claimed that US forces had executed them. As it turns out, I had attacked the "hospital" and the insurgents who were responsible for the video. By the time US forces arrived at the building days later, the enemy casualties had been removed but the insurgents had not had time to remove the evidence proving that they had used it as a staging location. Ultimately the charges were dropped and my team and I were cleared of any wrong doing. However, I will never forget Lieutenant Colonel Rainey's extraordinary leadership and my time with the 2-7 Cav.[198]

Going back to 10 November, the air missions continued in support of the battalion's fight. We were staying quite busy as the lead element of RCT-1 and the 1MARDIV and there were plenty of Muj' to choose from.

At 1600Z, Cougar and Apache pushed south of PL Fran to secure the Southwest sector of Fallujah. Comanche remained in place along PL Henry to provide security. During the 2-7 Cav's movement to contact, Toxin 42 remained established at the OP. While at the OP, Toxin 42 identified and engaged a three-man enemy RPG team with small arms. A few hours later, Toxin 42 observed a sniper team, an RPG team, and an observation team, believed to be the same team Toxin 42 engaged earlier, east of the intersection of Cathy and Henry monitoring 2-7 Cav movements. Despite their own safety, Toxin 42 risked exposing themselves to the sniper in order to maintain an optimal vantage point for controlling air strikes. Within minutes, Toxin 42 used Profane 43 (2 x F-18) to engage the enemy OP with a GBU-12, killing three enemy observers/spotters. Profane 43 reported multiple secondary explosions from the building and the streets surrounding the building. Still eyes on the sniper position, Toxin 42 had Profane 43 engaged the sniper position with two GBU-12s killing the three-man sniper team, a three-man RPG team and destroying the building that provided optimal viewing of 2-7 Cav movements.

During the push south along PL Henry, Toxin 40 used fixed wing assets to recce and clear Cougar's route of possible VBIEDs and obstructions. Once in place, Toxin 41 used Basher 75 to recce and destroy all

---

198 Gentile Jr.

targets along Cougar Company's route. (Toxin 41 is still in the field with Cougar Company).

Shortly after midnight on 11 Nov (early morning of 12 Nov), Cougar received battle damage and was forced to break contact. Unable to control from inside the Bradley, Toxin 41 transferred control of the AO to Toxin 40. Toxin 40 had Basher 74 engage multiple vehicles, 3 fortified fighting positions, and an enemy patrol aiding Comanche's recovery efforts. Basher 74's presence caused the insurgents to cease operations until daylight.

Around 0800Z, while on patrol, Comanche began taking fire from a building two blocks north of the intersection of PL Donna and George. Toxin 42 moved into a position to observe the location of the insurgents and quickly talked Dirty 63's eyes onto the target. Toxin 42 cleared Dirty 63 (2 x F-15E-Strike Eagle fighter jet) to put a GBU-12 on the target, ending the TIC.

Around 1300Z, the 3-1 Marines and 3-5 Marines secured the ground west of PL Henry from April to Jenna. The 2-7 Cav relinquished control of that battle space to RCT-1, whom retained control of the airspace and aircraft from that point on. Having been effectively removed from the fight, Toxin 40 began extracting the Toxin teams for recovery and re-outfit operations in preparation for the next mission. Toxin 41 remained in the field with Cougar Company, supporting the 2-7 Cav's main effort.[199]

At this time, the fight transitioned south of PL Fran and I began to rotate my FIST crews for rest, recovery, and refit. I was also able to ensure that all my Soldiers were given the opportunity to rotate duty between the front and the TOC. At this point, our battalion lost priority of fires and would now have to be more patient with our requests for both fires and air. Most of our efforts from that point on relied on our organic mortar fires, hence highest usage of any system by several

---

199 Ibid.

thousand rounds (not counting aircraft machine gun fire); however, we still had our moments. Mr. McAllester observed some of the southern Fallujah action.

> *Throughout the day, Rainey's intelligence* officers watched on a laptop screen the view from a drone gently flying over Shuhada. One soldier watched the live video feed, which shows what's happening on the ground in remarkable detail, while another communicated in a chat room with the Marine who was steering the drone. When they saw potential targets, they notified soldiers on the other side of the tent who called in the coordinates to artillery and mortar teams. One by one, they picked off a house that men carrying weapons were leaving and entering, a bus apparently being loaded with explosives, and seven cars, also being transformed into what the military calls VBIEDs — vehicle-borne improvised explosive devices. Each target evaporated in huge plumes as the shells landed.[200]

This break in the fight would afford Stroker and I the opportunity to do an in person on the ground in-depth battle damage assessment of our missions inside Fallujah. We were now in unplanned conditions. Our intended involvement in Operation Phantom Fury was supposed to have ended with our seizure of OBJs Pennsylvania, Virginia, Kentucky, and Ohio. We took the opportunity to assess our effects to date to ensure we adjusted, if need be, for the next phase of the battle, whatever that entailed. A historic and epic meeting was about to take place down south that would change the course of the fight for our battalion. Southern Fallujah, below PL Fran (Highway 10) was yet to be dealth with…

---

200 Matthew McAllester, "Assault on Fallujah," *Newsday*, November 12, 2004, A07.

8. BUGZAPPERS

How does one conquer fear of death, that most primordial of terrors, which resides in our very blood, as in all life, beasts as well as men? He indicated the hounds flanking Suicide. Dogs in a pack find courage to take on a lion. Each hound knows his place. He fears the dog ranked above and feeds off the fear of the dog below. Fear conquers fear. This is how we Spartans do it, counterpoising to fear of death a greater fear: that of dishonor. Of exclusion from the pack.[201]

—Steven Pressfield, *Gates of Fire*

11 NOVEMBER

Throughout the whole fight, the key leaders were on the ground staying in touch with the battle and with their units. In the words of Command Sgt. Maj. Mace, "The big boys actually got their feet dirty; they weren't hanging back moving stuff on a board."[202] In fact, he said he saw Col. Shupp and Maj. Gen. Natonski in the town daily and recalled what a good commander he thought Col. Shupp was and that, right off the bat, he just conveyed a mindset that "We're going to win!"[203] You could never underestimate the power of his positive attitude.

---

201 Pressfield, 231-32.
202 Mace, 2006, 191.
203 Ibid.

It was during one of these instances when all the commanders were getting their feet dirty down on the ground that the battle shifted from its original design. As the situation stood early on 11 November, 2-7 CAV and 3-1 Marines had pushed through the Jolan. RCT-7 on the east was almost online with RCT-1, but was having a much harder time. The plan had them attacking south and then sweeping from east to west, clearing the remaining southern half of the city. This presented a decision point for the 1MARDIV Commander, Maj. Gen. Natonksi. He happened to have two men with him that could offer their assessment and give him the information he needed to decide on a course of action.

There are several versions of what happened next and all of them together are probably about as close to the truth as you can get. Consequently, Maj. Gen. Natonksi, Col. Shupp, and Lt. Col. Rainey are having a meeting of the minds on hotly contested PL Henry (near another fortified mosque fighting position) out in the open to discuss the future of the battle. It could not have been a more iconic image. Maj. Gen. Natonski recalls talking to Jim (Rainey) and Mike (Shupp) and asking, "What do you think if we pulled Jim Rainey and moved him to the other side of the city to support the RCT-7 attack? Then they would continue on, based on our initial plan."[204] According to Maj. Gen. Natonski, Lt. Col. Rainey responded, "Garryowen, I can do it," and he thought to himself, "That's what I'd expect a Marine to say."[205]

Col. Shupp remembers informing Maj. Gen. Natonski that, "Hey, we're already at our objectives. We should just keep on going."[206] Of course, he and Maj. Gen. Natonski had probably already discussed keeping 2-7 CAV with RCT-1, but with no final decision made. So here they are, continuing the discussion standing at a mosque in downtown Fallujah discussing this with dead enemy fighters laying around, enemy snipers trying to shoot them, their missed shots knocking tiles onto their

---

204 Natonski, 2007, 7.
205 Ibid.
206 Shupp, 2006, 60.

helmets from the minaret looming above them.[207] Maj. Gen. Natonski then says to Lt. Col. Rainey, "I want you to go to 7th Marines" and Lt. Col. Rainey responded, "I'd rather stay with 1st Marines. I'd rather stay with Inchon."[208] Maj. Gen. Natonski then looks back at Col. Shupp and says, "Could you keep going to the south of the city?" to which Col. Shupp replied, "Absolutely, sir, but we need Jim Rainey to stay with us."[209] The reason to consider continuing to push the enemy to the south was the idiom of the hammer and the anvil, of "combined Army and Marine units…to keep pushing the insurgents south, killing as many as possible along the way, until they [had] been swept into the southern reaches of the city, where more American forces awaited them."[210] Lt. Col. Rainey recollects telling Maj. Gen. Natonski that it would not be

> …*easy to break contact, disengage,* get back and go get integrated in a new regimental combat team, so I offered the suggestion of just continuing the attack south along Phase Line Henry. It would just be easier, purely from a re-task organization perspective for 2-7.[211]

Lt. Col. Rainey remembered the rest of the conversation being private between Col. Shupp and Maj. Gen. Natonski.[212] The result, however, was that RCT-1 would take the western half of the southern portion of the city. RCT-7 would take the eastern half, thereby equally splitting the city in half from north to south. The plan was going to be the same as it was for the Jolan. C/3-8 CAV would attack along PL Henry and from east to west into the enemy flanks. A/2-7 CAV would attack along several avenues north to south into the heart of the Nazal and Shuha-

---

207 Ibid., 60-61.
208 Ibid., 61.
209 Ibid.
210 McAllester, "Guerilla's Paradise," A03.
211 Rainey, 2006, 126-27.
212 Ibid., 127.

da Districts, more commonly referred to as Martyrs, disrupting enemy command and control and destroying large pockets of enemy resistance (see map below). Matt McAllester explained,

> *It's called the neighborhood of* the Martyrs, a warren of narrow streets and interconnected buildings. Until last night, American forces had not ventured in. That changed when all three companies of the heavily armored 2nd Battalion of the 7th Cavalry Regiment drove through the northern half of the city, crossed the main east-west road in the center and pushed into this southwestern sector of Fallujah. Abrams tanks roared through the dusty streets. Bradley Fighting Vehicles rattled alongside, their gun turrets swiveling, searching for the enemy. Contrary to some reports, much of Fallujah is not under the control of U.S. and Iraqi government forces. Most of the entire southern half had not been probed before last night. That left U.S. commanders with a question: Is the resistance weaker than expected so far because the insurgents have fled the city, were overestimated to begin with, or have pulled back from the northwestern neighborhoods to the south? "Worst case is the enemy fell all the way to the south and are waiting for us," said Lt. Col. Jim Rainey, commanding officer of the 2nd Battalion, as he briefed his officers yesterday morning in his command tent just outside Fallujah. As on the second night of the battle—the first day of major combat—it was the 2nd Battalion that led the way, riding in tanks and Bradleys and blasting the way for Marine infantrymen, who go door-to-door in the hunt for insurgents who have survived the initial onslaught.[213]

---

213 McAllester, "Assault on Fallujah," A07.

Source: Gott, Kendall D. and John McCool
Eyewitness to War: The US Army in Operation Al Fajr, an Oral History
Fort Leavenworth, KS: Combat Studies Institute Press, 2006.

12-19 NOVEMBER

The fight for the Martyrs' neighborhoods and the southwestern section of Fallujah was distinctive. Early intelligence reports portrayed a different enemy disposition. Enemy contact in the southern part of Fallujah was going to be a lot heavier. 1st Lt. Erwin thought that possibly the first few days of fighting in the northern section of the Jolan had caused a large portion of the Muj' to give ground there because they wanted nothing to do with the heavy armor of the tanks and Bradleys.[214] The enemy anticipated a majority of our force to be dismounted, similar to the April Operation Vigilant Resolve, and when it was not, they retreated south to make a last stand, hoping that maybe the armor would not come that far.[215]

Other notions attributed the lighter contact in the north due to the shaping operations of the Marines days and weeks before the battle that convinced the insurgents that the eventual assault had to be coming from the south. Therefore, the enemy had placed all the best fighters in positions in southern Fallujah and the least reliable in the northern areas. We heard unsubstantiated reports from interpreters that identified many of the Muj' in southern Fallujah as insurgents from Syria, Russia, Saudi Arabia, and Lebanon.[216] Enemy tactics were also revealing as Mr. McAllester attested,

> *One thing more than any* other convinced the 2nd Battalion and other U.S. forces early in the day that the forces they were now fighting in the south of the city are the hardcore of Fallujah's insurgents: They were using expensive and up-to-date armor-piercing rocket-propelled grenades, or RPGs, and they knew how to fire them accurately and in complex ambush formation. That implied considerable financial resources, efficient arms supplies, and military experience and training. It had some military commanders wondering whether the rumors of expert Chechen rebels working as commanders in Fallujah might be true.[217]

This led us to believe that the enemy in the Nazal and Shuhada Dis-

---

214 Erwin, 2006, 54-55.
215 Ibid., 55.
216 Twaddell, 2006, 136.
217 McAllester, "Guerilla's Paradise," A03.

tricts was a bit smarter, better trained, semi-professional, and more dangerous. Lt. Col. Rainey altered the battalion's tactics slightly due to the
shifting dynamics of the environment and threat.

After the first push down a north-south main road the Americans have named Henry, his men reached their goals in the Jolan
neighborhood ahead of schedule. They then had to wait longer
than expected for the Marines to sweep in behind. That left the
2nd Battalion vulnerable as they waited in captured buildings.
"I hated it," Rainey said. "We kept going and the enemy leaked
around the sides," he told his officers. "That's OK." This time, his
tanks and Bradleys were going in, doing their job and getting
out by sunrise. "Maintain 360-degree security," he said. "Destroy
everything you can destroy. Make sure you keep together." He
reminded his officers of the Rules of Engagement that are de-
signed to protect civilians — "We're not murderers," he warned
them — but the message was clear: "Given those constraints, kill
everything you can kill." He continued: "The Marines are having a tough fight. I don't want them to have a catastrophic fight.
Those roadside bombs, car bombs, IEDs [improvised explosive
devices] and 55-gallon drums — those kids can't see that. So
pound those roads."[218]

Intelligence preparation of the battlefield was critical to the fight for
southern Fallujah. It was also done with much less time available to prepare compared to the Jolan (remember the complete change in the plan).
Capt. Gray and 1st Lt. Erwin with their intelligence section; however,
did not leave us wanting for terrain and enemy assessments.

During the briefing in the dirty tent strung between armored ve-

218 McAllester, "Assault on Fallujah," A07.

hicles, radios crackling and generators grumbling in the background, Rainey's intelligence officer, Capt. David Gray, explained what he knew about the Martyrs, or Shuhada, district. Using a PowerPoint presentation on a laptop computer that matched the photocopied handouts in each officer's hands, Gray described a neighborhood of tall, close buildings. On an aerial photograph, most of its roads were colored red, meaning they were 15 feet wide or less. If you go down a road like that, Gray warned, there's only one way out. No turning around and coming back.... He described [the] number of insurgents as "significant."...The architecture and urban layout of the Shuhada district offered terrain "denser than what we're used to," he continued. The secondary roads are "not nearly as good as what we're used to." While "potentially tankable," he said, "any given part of that road could be a significant choke." The goal was to be out by sunrise, Rainey told his officers, to allow the Marines to move in." We're going to make it easier for them," explained his operations officer, Maj. Tim Karcher.[219]

Word made it to and spread throughout the southern half of the city of more effective tactics, techniques and procedures to use against our forces as the battle continued. The enemy had a vote. We adjusted and so did they. Many of these new insurgents resorted to chemical alternatives to help as well; hopped up on drugs, evidenced by dead insurgents with tourniquets on with syringes of Novocain and adrenaline, were found throughout the area.[220] They were planning to fight to the death wherever we found them-no surrender. Their plan was to hole up (stay hidden) inside buildings with deadly defenses and booby traps waiting for Marines or Soldiers to enter and then kill them in an ambush. They would stay there, not coming out, forcing another group of reinforcing

---

219 Ibid.
220 Shupp, 2006, 62.

Marines or Soldiers to clear the building, hoping to kill them, too. And so on, and so on, until we killed them all. This tactic gave rise to the term "hell house;" places that were effectively hell on earth and very costly to eliminate—the price being many American lives. With the nature of the fight shifting and in a fluid state, there were some concerns about moving south.

> *While it is unquestionably true* that U.S. and Iraqi forces have moved with relative ease and speed throughout the northern half of the city, encountering less resistance than anticipated, the insurgents have an almost liquid ability to shift position. That makes killing them a slow business, and it makes it impossible for commanders to know whether the insurgents are being picked off in proportionately large numbers or whether they are slipping through the lines to other parts of town. The south, until last night, was the uncharted territory of Fallujah. When night had fallen, the Bradleys of Apache Company loaded up. Lt. Dan Kilgore, leader of the 1st Platoon, said, "The problem is they keep going south. Now we are going into the deep, deep jungle."[221]

The enemy did not want to fight in limited visibility anymore, due to our advantage in night optics, which made purely nighttime operations less effective. During the day, they were less likely to come out and attack our positions unless it was worth it. The Muj' wanted us to work our way deep into the irregular and confusing maze of Martyrs and root them out-house by bloody house. We in turn employed a few new tactics of our own to counter this shift by the enemy.

Lt. Col. Rainey likened it to being "bugzappers."[222] We would present our vehicles during daylight (the enemy spent the night hiding) enticing them to reveal their location by drawing fire and then bring all

---

221 McAllester, "Assault on Fallujah," A07.
222 McAllester, "Guerilla's Paradise," A03.

the heavy combat power to bear before Marines had to deal with them. In Najaf the battalion learned, "if you park it, they will come...We got down there...We found the bugs. We're killing them."[223] This idea was a tactic based upon a well thought out and calculated risk. Our equipment, our numbers, and our skilled warriors against anything the enemy could throw at us. "I knew we could take the RPG shots and four tanks/BFVs scanning and with good interlocking fires allowed us to make contact and kill enemy that would otherwise have been waiting in buildings for the Marines," expressed Col Rainey* after the battle.[224]

Lt. Col. Rainey (left) and Capt. Glass (right) confer during a break in the fighting
Source: Photo courtesy of Eric Hough.

After the enemy initiated attacks with RPGs and mortars, in most cases, Capt. Chaos would close with and destroy the enemy with his tank

---

223 Ibid.
224 James Rainey, July 15, 2012.

*At the time of this email communication he was a full-bird Colonel, promoted since the battle.

led "mini thunder runs" (essentially fast-striking armored raids against enemy forces). [225] With the mission the Marines gave us, the environment of the battlefield, and the condition of our battalion, the cost benefit analysis of the bugzapper tactic no doubt saved lives. Lt. Gen. Moore would say Lt. Col. Rainey "[did] not accept very much risk that [was] out of [his] control. [His] brain calculate[d] risk in a different more important way...Intuition! The feeling in [his] bones. [He] tuned into that voice."[226] Not every commander has that ability, but I thank God everyday Lt. Col. Rainey did, otherwise Fallujah might have been worse.

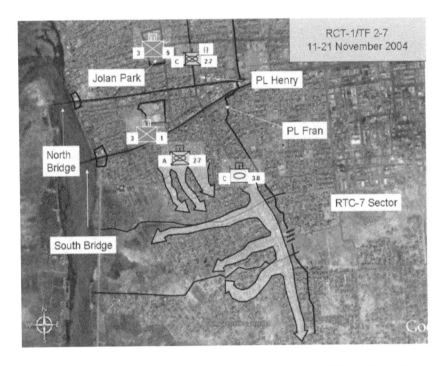

Source: Matthews, Matt. *Operation Al Fajr: A Study in Army and Marine Corps Joint Operations.* Fort Leavenworth, KS: Combat Studies Institute, 2006.

225 Glass, 2006, 77.
226 Moore, 13.

Matt McAllester described the scene in Fallujah as attacks commenced in the south on or about 12 November.

The center of Fallujah is a shattered place. Rotting bodies in the street fill the air with the stench of death, which comes and goes with the breeze. Chunks of rubble are strewn along roads and sidewalks. Many stores and homes and other cinderblock buildings have huge holes ripped into them by American shells. Bombs have collapsed many roofs. The electric and telephone wires that line the streets are now twisted spaghetti. There's no power in town and the moon is a mere sliver right now, so at night, the only thing that lights up the streets is the glow of speeding munitions and explosions. Cats and dogs are the only casual pedestrians in town. On Thursday night, soldiers in one Bradley watched on their infrared screen as three dogs, showing up as dark figures in the green-and-black world of infrared, tore at the flesh of a dead body. War-torn Fallujah is a guerrilla's paradise. The rubble and the darkened holes of the town's abandoned shells provide great cover. Narrow alleyways and tight-knit housing help their movement. They appear, shoot, and disappear. Actually spotting them is a rarity for most soldiers. "It was like a shooting gallery at a carnival," said Capt. Ed Twaddell, 30, the commander of Apache company, Friday afternoon. "They pop up, they pop down." With the fighting increasing in tempo, Twaddell, the other company commanders, and Rainey decided to initiate a two-pronged attack in a fresh piece of territory south of a road the Americans have named Isabel.[227]

On 12 November, while Capt. Twaddell's Alpha Company plus a portion of Cougar Company was consolidated to allow for an air mission

---

227 McAllester, "Guerilla's Paradise," A03.

and some refit after bugzapping, they started receiving a heavy amount of mortar fire.[228] Capt. Twaddell decided that instead of waiting on an airstrike and eating mortars [siting in place taking the brunt of the attack] for an unknown period of time, he would maneuver on the enemy, close with, and then destroy them.[229] Ghost 5 approved of the action and told Ed, "Hey, you're the man. Go."[230] As Ed began to move, his element came under heavy direct fire and the attack was halted by a direct hit on the rear of his Bradley by some form of armor piercing RPG. Capt. Twaddell recalled,

> *The RPG penetrated below the* right hand gun port, sheared off Sergeant Newman's arm, passed right through Izzy, passed underneath the screen for the Force XXI Battle Command, Brigade-and-Below [FBCB2] system and penetrated the turret through the turret shield. We had the turret slewed...The penetrator passed through the turret shield into the ammo ready box and detonated a couple of high explosive [HE] rounds. How Sergeant Queen and I didn't catch any shrapnel, I have no clue.[231]

1st Lts. Mike Duran, Dan Kilgore, and Matt Wojcik proceeded to form a perimeter around the damaged Bradley of Apache 6 and suppress the enemy.[232] One of the tanks that came to support pulled up right behind Apache 60 and was hit with a mortar, wounding Spc. Brian Svendsen, (he would earn two Purple Hearts during the battle).[233] Lt. Col. Rainey remembers thinking at the time that this sounded a lot like a *Black Hawk Down* kind of incident, but due to some unbelievable her-

---

228 Twaddell, 2006, 132.
229 Ibid.
230 Ibid.
231 Ibid., 133.
232 Rainey, 2006, 128.
233 Glass, 2006, 76.

oism on the part of some young Soldiers, it did not turn out that way.[234] Capt. Twaddell recalled PSG Calvin Smalley helping direct the fire of the company dismounts as Spc. Scott "Doc" Cogil began treating the casualties.[235] Izzy, the interpreter was KIA, Tactical Psyop Team, Sgt. Brian Newman, lost his left arm right below the shoulder, and both Sgt. Delhotal and Spc. Rankin received shrapnel wounds.[236] After the attack, the company took care of the casualties, refueled, rearmed, and refitted, not skipping a beat so they could be back down south in the fight in just a few hours. Matt McAllester documented the attack.

At noon, Apache 14 had joined a group of other armored vehicles near the courtyard and three-story building. Suddenly, fire seemed to be coming from all sides. "Apache 60's been hit," came a tense voice over the radio. …There were casualties, the voice said. "They need evac immediately." Cogil knew that meant he was up. He was the closest medic to the scene. Sitting in the back of a Bradley Fighting Vehicle, Apache 14, only 50 yards from the Bradley that had just taken a vicious hit from another armor-piercing RPG, 20-year-old Cogil jammed his Kevlar helmet onto his head, grabbed his aid bag and waited for the ramp at the back of the tracked vehicle to lower. So did four other soldiers, waiting in the near-dark box they had been sitting in for 18 hours, crawling around the streets of Fallujah while the gunner blasted away at insurgents. With the hum of hydraulics, the ramp started going down. Their faces were tight. For all they knew, some of them, perhaps all of them, might not come back. They didn't discuss what they had to do in those moments as sunlight flooded the vehicle; not a word. The ramp hit the ground and outside there were hundreds of bullets flying around.… Their M-16

234 Rainey, 2006, 127.
235 Twaddell, 2006, 134.
236 Ibid., 133.

rifles pointing toward nearby buildings, the five young soldiers burst out into a confusing world of noon light, massive gunfire, hidden enemies, and injured comrades. They didn't even know which of the other nearby Bradleys they were meant to run to. They found it. There was a hole in the rear of Apache 60. Small, about an inch in diameter, but big enough for the grenade to enter the tiny compartment that can fit six soldiers. It had crashed through, searing through the side of an Iraqi-American translator, ripping the left arm off one of the soldiers almost at the shoulder and leaving shrapnel embedded in two others. Blinding smoke mixed with blood in an instant. Twaddell was in the turret. Soft-spoken, bespectacled and modest, he kept his nerve in the chaos. "It was very confusing," he said later. "I saw a flash in front of my knee. The turret was filled with smoke. I checked the gunner was OK, popped the hatch." Twaddell stuck to his radio while his men tended to the wounded. Within minutes, he had organized a group of Bradleys around Apache 60 and Cogil and the other four from Apache 14 were there to help. Bullets cracked past them and they didn't really know where they were coming from. Everywhere, it seemed. Cogil found the wounded sergeant already lifted out of the Bradley, a soldier holding his belt tightly around the bleeding stump as a tourniquet. Fortunately, the arm was severed so far up that the major artery in the upper arm was not blown open. Cogil applied a more permanent tourniquet and helped load the wounded soldier into another Bradley. "He was taking it like a champ, saying 'I'm fine, I'm fine,'" said Cogil, of Rantoul, Ill. The wounded sergeant kept asking if his men were safe as they rushed him out of the kill zone. On the way, Cogil said, boxes of ammunition and other items kept falling on the wounded man. "I felt terrible," Cogil said.[237]

---

237 McAllester, "Guerilla's Paradise," A03.

Capt. Twaddell in action in Fallujah
Source: Photo courtesy of Eric Hough.

Capt. Chaos with his tandem bugzapping and mini thunder runs were an immense help to the Marines during this time. The whole purpose in offering the tactic to the Marines was in an effort to help reduce their casualties. We felt that we could be of more use than we were, so we offered them a solution. If they let us know what their operations were for the next day then we would conduct some of our runs into the area before they had to send in Marines. We wanted them to know that we were still an option.

Capt. Chris Brooke continued to secure and keep PL Henry open as our LOC, and was also doing quite a bit of Marine casualty evacuation because it was "the right thing to do."[238] Chris remembered, "At times it would happen right before our crew's eyes. A section would control an intersection and mortars would begin falling on a group of Marines getting ready to enter a building. We'd grab them in the backs of our Bradleys and run them back to the train station."[239] Continually removing Marine casualties one after the other made us feel awful and want to do something more to improve their circumstances. When and where it was possible, Cougar and Apache Company's efforts were having very positive results. So much so that after single runs, tanks were having to go rearm at the TFSA because they had shot so many main tank rounds.

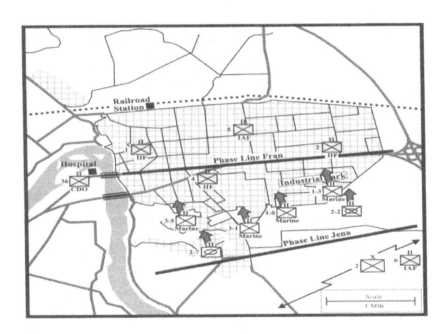

Source: Gott, Kendall D. and John McCool, *Eyewitness to War: The US Army in Operation Al Fajr, an Oral History.* Fort Leavenworth, KS
Combat Studies Institute Press, 2006.

---

238 Brooke, 2006, 275-76.
239 Ibid.

The battalion; however, felt it could do more. Maj. Karcher commented, "We were just maintaining Route Henry, isolating the area and letting the Marines do the fighting—and the Marines were taking far greater casualties than we thought were necessary or required."[240] Therefore, Lt. Col. Rainey and Maj. Karcher made the Marines an offer.

Hey, look we can do some stuff for you. If you'll tell us what your ops are for tomorrow, before the sun comes up we can just drive through there, attempt to draw out any fire, and destroy some of those strong points before you have to send men in first.[241]

Sometime after 12 November, Maj.Karcher received a call from the 3-1 Marines S3 (operations officer) wanting him to swing by the train station after filling up with fuel and ammunition on his way back into the city.[242] Maj. Karcher recollects as soon as they swung into the station and dismounted their Bradleys, the 3-1 Marines Commander (Lt. Col. Willy Buhl) and S3 (Maj. Christeon Griffin) walked up to Lt. Col. Rainey and himself, gave them both a big hug, and said, "That was awesome, man! We went into the buildings and there was nothing but freaking dead insurgents in there."[243] The Marines and our battalion had reached the southern edge of Fallujah and did an about face (180 degree turn) and began working our way back north. This process lasted for about four or five more days before the battle started to wind down. In southern Fallujah, we may have helped save many Marine lives, but in the process, we lost some of our own.

---

240 Karcher, 2006, 206.
241 Ibid.
242 Ibid.
243 Ibid.

9. THE PRICE

When a warrior fights not for himself, but for his brothers, when his most passionately sought goal is neither glory nor his own life's preservation, but to spend his substance for them, his comrades, not to abandon them, not to prove unworthy of them, then his heart truly has achieved contempt for death, and with that he transcends himself and his actions touch the sublime. This is why the true warrior cannot speak of battle save to his brothers who have been there with him. This truth is too holy, too sacred for words.[244]　　　　　　　　　　　—Steven Pressfield, *Gates of Fire*

12-13 NOVEMBER

The battle for Fallujah in the late fall of 2004 was probably going as well as anyone could have asked for, considering the ferociousness of the fighting. 2-7 CAV, however, was not invincible. No matter what a piece of paper may have said about the disparity between our forces and that of the enemy in Fallujah, they were deadly, very deadly. The outcome was never in doubt, but as Command Sgt. Maj. Mace said after the battle, "We knew we were going to get where we were going to go, the question was just how long was it going to take us and how bad were we going to get hurt."[245] We did get hurt.

---

244 Pressfield, 332.
245 Mace, 2006, 188.

We lost six tanks during the battle, which says a lot about just how viciously the enemy was fighting back. There were two penetrations of number one skirts (covers on the side of the tank that partially shield the track), one track was blown off by a mine, there were several deep penetrations of the front hull armor, some weapon systems damaged and a main gun took an RPG through the tube.[246] When Capt. Chaos hit a Brazilian mine with his tank it lifted the tank up, knocked out all communication, blew the track and road wheels off, and penetrated the turret near the loader and ammunition rack.[247]

The battalion also lost three or four Bradleys to battle damage as well. The equipment was easily replaceable with the great support we received from our parent units; in fact, our organic Brigade Commander, Col. John Murray, even offered replacement vehicles to us with crews if we needed them.[248] Losing equipment was not difficult to deal with; losing Soldiers was a different story.

We lost two Soldiers while in Fallujah. Our first was Sgt. Jonathan Shields from Atlanta, Georgia. On 12 November, SGT Shields's tank was hit by an RPG wounding several crew members and also causing damage to the main gun. Staff Sgt. Reyes, the tank commander, made the smart choice to take the tank to the battalion aid station (BAS) and drop off the casualties and then on to the TFSA as it was not functioning properly due to the attack damage.[249] Staff Sgt. Reyes and Spc. Modeste were transferred to the BAS and Sgt. Shields, although wounded himself took on the responsibility of being the tank commander with Spc. Troy Caicedo driving, and headed for the TFSA to get the tank fixed and back into the fight.[250]

The tank commander's hatch in the turret was damaged in the attack so Sgt. Shields was riding partly out of the hatch so he could see (it was

---

246 Rainey, 2006, 120.
247 Glass, 2006, 79.
248 Rainey, 2006, 132.
249 Glass, 2006, 78.
250 Ibid., 78-79.

late at night around 2300).[251] On the way back, the tank slipped off the trail down into a 60-foot strip mine to the north of the train station that no one knew was there.[252] Sgt. Shields was killed instantly when he was caught between the ground and the top of the tank.

Command Sgt. Maj. Mace recalls as a Platoon Sergeant in the Gulf War he never had a KIA or lost a Soldier; Jonathan Shields was his first.[253] Maj. Karcher, Command Sgt. Maj. Mace, and the Physician's Assistant (PA) went forward to the accident site after the TOC got a call that we had a flipped over tank and a possible casualty.[254] As they got there the tank was inverted and at the bottom of the ravine with the back deck on fire.[255] There was no way to tell if anyone was hurt until the maintenance recovery team got there and lifted and righted the tank. Once they moved the tank, Sgt. Shields was lying on the ground. Maj. Karcher, Command Sgt. Maj. Mace and a few others recovered Sgt. Shields' body. Jonathan Shields was the first Ghost we lost. Unfortunately, and definitely not callously, Command Sgt. Maj. Mace reminded us, "This is war, kids get hurt."[256] The mission remained and the danger was still clear and present.

The fight continued; but losses, both killed and wounded, along with the stress of combat wore on the battalion. Our unit had Chaplain Jonathon Fowler whose impact cannot be understated in maintaining Ghost members' spiritual health. Like all good Chaplains, he came to the point of need, where the Soldiers were...in Fallujah itself. One such encounter was Chaplain Fowler

> ...*tending to the spirits of* young men who have to go through things most people never have to deal with as long as they live...

---

251 Rainey, 2006, 128; Mace, 2006, 189.
252 Rainey, 2006, 128.
253 Mace, 2006, 189.
254 Ibid.
255 Ibid.
256 Ibid.

after walking around the resting troops, he held a short Sunday service in the dirty, battered kitchen of the house. Amid the killing, some talk of love. A dozen soldiers gathered round Fowler, a man who seems to remember every soldier's name without hesitation. He will often grab a soldier's hand and put his hand on their shoulder, calling them "my friend." He asked the gathered troops for prayer requests. "Families back home," one said. There was a pause. "Fellow warriors?" prompted Fowler. "Guys that have been hurt," came a voice. "Anything else?"

"Sgt. Shields' family," someone said. "Everyone fighting here," someone else said.

Once all the requests were in, Fowler prayed for them, holding his left hand in the air.

"Watch over them, shroud them in your love," he asked his God. He then read Philippians 4:13 from his camouflaged Bible: "I can do everything through him who gives me strength." After the final "Amen," Sgt. Coy Embry, 24, from Norman, Okla., stood quietly at the side. "It gives the guys a chance to maybe get away," he said, of the prayer service. "Gets their minds off the killing and brutality of war to what's more important in life, family back home and getting home."[257]

The next day, 13 November, did not get any better. The battalion suffered another casualty after having just lost Sgt. Shields and dealt with the vicious attack on Apache 60 where we lost an interpreter, Sgt. Newman lost his arm, and we had two other wounded in action the day prior. About 1130 on 13 November, Apache Company, was still standing tall down in the Martyrs, taking the fight to the enemy despite the previous events. 1st Platoon came into contact and Staff Sgt. Santillana's squad dismounted to pursue an insurgent fighter spotted running across an

---

257 McAllester, "Pockets of Resistance," A04.

alley into a building where approximately 10-20 insurgents were lying in wait.[258] Alpha Company was about to come face to face with one of Fallujah's hell houses. Mr. McAllester described the personal cruelty of war.

A 2-7 CAV infantry squad on the move inside Fallujah
Source: Photo courtesy of Eric Hough

When the fighting began, the 2nd Battalion of the 7th Cavalry was the tool that punched the hole in Fallujah. That's what they were there for. The Army battalion's Abrams tanks and Bradley Fighting Vehicles destroy with an efficiency and ferocity unmatched by the limited firepower of the Marines, who have a comparatively small number of armored vehicles. Staff Sgt. Carlos Santillana's squad of eight men arrived early on Tuesday morning, eight days ago, in the heart of the insurgent stronghold of Jolan, a neigh-

<hr>

258 Twaddell, 2006, 135.

borhood in the northwest of the city. His company, Apache, was ahead of schedule and so it took over a group of school buildings next to a small park. The plan was that the Marines would then catch up and start moving, house to house, block by block, killing or capturing insurgents. That evening, Santillana's men could be forgiven for thinking that someone, somewhere, had it in for them. By Saturday, only two of the eight were still standing. Five lay on stretchers and one was sheathed in a body bag. "That's war," Santillana would say days later, his world clouded by sadness, no longer the quick-talking, wise-cracking dynamo he had been before the battle. "That's all I can say."[259]

The squad entered and secured a foothold in the courtyard, prepped the entryway with a grenade and kicked in the door.[260] The enemy had built a bunker inside the house, allowing them to survive the initial entry blast and then opened fire on the squad with an RPK (Russian-Ruchnoy Pulemyot Kalashnikova) light machine gun, inflicting five casualties in moments.[261] While the squad was getting the wounded to safety, they started receiving sniper fire and grenades being thrown on them from above.[262] This ordeal transpired in just a few moments as Mr. McAllester explains.

Finally, Santillana's squad came to a two-story gray house. It looked suspicious. Perhaps it was just a feeling, perhaps it was because all the other homes around were smarter, more expensive-looking. So, they threw a grenade over the wall into the courtyard and one into the house. Then they rushed in, with Abe, ever the point man, kicking the door down. "Oh, —," San-

---

259 Matthew McAllester, "Band of Brothers," *Newsday*, November 17, 2004, A05.
260 Twaddell, 2006, 135.
261 Rainey, 2006, 128.
262 Ibid.

tillana heard Abe shout, and an instant later there was a huge burst of gunfire from inside the house, several weapons firing at once. "We were shooting everywhere," Santillana said yesterday. "Sergeant Abe came crawling out the door, he was just covered in blood." Santillana told another of the men to grab Abe and get him out of there. The soldier did so, but as he was pulling Abe out by the collar straps he "half spun around." Shot in the shoulder, the soldier nevertheless grabbed Abe again and kept pulling. Another soldier threw a grenade into the house. All the time, Santillana said, Velez stood shooting into the house. Two grenades came back out at the men, injuring another two. "Velez still stood," Santillana said, "pumping away…Velez moved back out into the street, shooting into the house. He told us to go." It was chaotic. Different members of the squad were now wounded, some lying on top of each other, some still standing and fighting, others diving for cover. Now there was another insurgent shooting from behind them. Cogil was taking cover and looked at Velez, who had finished the rounds in his magazine. "I need to reload," he called out, Cogil recalled. The next time Cogil and Santillana, from their different positions, looked at Velez, he was face down on the ground, motionless. Santillana has no memory of it, but he's been told that all that time he was yelling into his radio for help from the nearby Bradleys and tanks. It took them only minutes to arrive. "This all happened in less than three or four minutes," Santillana said. "It was just a mad minute of hell."[263]

The point man, Sgt. Abdelwahab was hit immediately in the right leg and left arm and the number two man, Spc. Howard grabbed his wounded squad mate and pulled him back out of the kill zone.[264] At that time, Spc. Jose Velez was using his SAW (small squad automatic

---

263 McAllester, "Band of Brothers," A05.
264 Twaddell, 2006, 135.

machine gun) to suppress the enemy and protect his buddies, of which three were now wounded. There was also a sniper across the street, firing on the squad, and he hit Spc. Velez in the neck. When Spc. Velez went down, Spc. Benny Alicea picked up the suppressive fire and their actions together allowed enough time to begin the CASEVAC.[265] Velez and Alicea's covering fire and actions allowed the squad to disengage and get to safety. The significance of their heroism in protecting their squad earned them both the Silver Star.[266] 1st Lt. Matt Wojcik's 3rd Platoon of tanks arrived and blasted the house with a section's worth of main tank rounds.[267]

By that time, the CASEVAC was headed back north to the BAS where the PA, Capt. Kevin Burnham, and his medics were waiting. The two most seriously wounded were stabilized; two others with less severe wounds were bandaged and treated, but Spc. Velez had succumbed to his wound. All the wounded left for follow-on medical care on MEDEVAC helicopters. Matt McAllester witnessed the scene's conclusion.

As they were loading up the casualties, another grenade thrown by the insurgents injured yet another member of the squad. There was a lot of blood and a lot of bleeding in the two Bradleys as they charged north through Fallujah to the 2nd Battalion's temporary base just north of the city at an old plaster works. There, the battalion's medical team stabilized the living. Abe was bleeding profusely from the artery on the inside of his thigh. The day before, after racing back safely from the rescue mission, he had sat in the back of the quiet Bradley and said, "It's not my time." It still wasn't. It was Jose Velez's time.... Abe lay on a stretcher on Saturday morning in the shade provided by the medical tent, a buddy holding a cigarette to his quivering lips.

---

265 Rainey, 2006, 128.
266 Ibid.
267 Ibid.

The corn-flour-fine dust of the desert north of Fallujah puffed in the breeze around him. His right knee was bound up, his left hand deformed perhaps for life, a doctor said, and for once Abdelwahab, just when he had proved his courage beyond doubt, wasn't playing the hero. "I ain't gonna lie to you, buddy," he said, looking up from his stretcher. "It hurts like a —." Cogil looked down at the man whose life he had just helped save. And at another three soldiers from the same squad, all lying on stretchers in the shade, waiting for the helicopters to arrive. One had his head propped up on his helmet, sobbing quietly as a buddy held his head, pressing his forehead against the injured man's. Spc. Benny Alicea lay silent, staring at the sky. Goodin was laughing and grinning a bit manically, calling out about how he was going to have ice cream, his left knee now holding several pieces of metal. Usually wise-cracking, riffing on any theme he could grab in his fluid, hilarious, Southern story-telling way, the squad's leader walked with a stoop of grief. Santillana looked pale as he bent down to talk with his old friend Abe. "What's up, brother?" he asked. Abdelwahab managed a wobbly grin and gave a brief description of what had happened in a house in Fallujah barely an hour before. "I shot that — in the head, though," was the way he finished the short account. Cogil walked past them all and pulled aside the dark khaki flap to the aid tent, which had been deliberately closed so other soldiers could not see what was inside. On a raised cot to the right lay a black body bag.... With the calm of an elderly surgeon who has seen it all before, his face showing nothing but gentleness, he moved to the side of the bag and unzipped it all the way. Inside lay the body of Spc. Jose Velez, 23, still in his uniform. His usually wide eyes were narrowed to frozen slits, his frequent and broad grin now just a slim parting of the lips. Cogil pulled down Velez's shirt and looked at the bullet wound below his friend's neck. He examined it closely but briefly. "Is that what got him?" he asked another medic. Yes, was the answer. "Thank you," Cogil said, zipping up the bag. He walked out into the November sunshine. "I wanted to make sure that's what it was, that there was no chance," he said. "I put him on the bottom. All I could do was hold his hand. Just pray the whole way back. Just worked on Sergeant Abe 'cause I could see he was bleeding all the way down his pants." Cogil took a can of Coke. Then he walked over to talk privately with the battalion's chaplain, Capt. Jonathan Fowler. Finally, his face changed. Cogil bowed his head, and his face crumpled into tears.[268]

Our casualties were special, like so many others that were lost in Fallujah. Sgt. Shields died fully committed to his fellow Soldiers and his mission, doing his best to get his tank fixed and back to his company or get on another tank because he knew how important the outcome of the battle was. Spc. Velez died in the act of protecting his brothers in the squad, putting himself in harm's way to ensure no one would get trapped in that hell house. Not all the noble causes and heroic deeds in the world makes losses in war any easier to bear, just ask Staff Sgt. Santillana.

Carlos Santillana was lonely... he had been the last man standing from his squad when the shooting was over on Saturday morning. On Monday evening, he sat on an upturned cinder block on the front porch of Apache Company's temporary base. "I only got one guy [Price] left from my squad, everybody else is gone. You turn to your left, you turn to the right...I sit in the back of a Bradley and it's no one I'm used to working with." He does know them, his new squad, from the platoon; but it's not the team he'd helped to mold into a close-knit unit, a tiny fraternity with its shared jokes and intimacies. "Under the present circum-

---

268 McAllester, "Band of Brothers," A05.

stances," he said, "I think I'm doing all right." Immediately after his soldiers had been flown away in two helicopters on Saturday morning, Santillana felt lost. "Sat by myself, cried a lot," he said, his thin face newly pale, his liquid talk lost for now. "It's just…uh…kinda…replayed over and over…what happened, in my head. And it scares the — out of me every time I think about it. All I did was to ask the chaplain to pray with me, pray for Spc. Velez, pray for his wife, that she finds peace somewhere. It's not going to be easy. It's never easy."[269]

Capt. Twaddell recalls visiting with the squad before they were airlifted to the rear and remembers having never, "seen anybody [Santillana] feel as guilty, I think about that. He loved his men, and I think he felt like he should be lying there in the medical tent with them."[270] Staff Sgt. Santillana while standing at the side of Spc. Velez said he did not "open the bag. I basically knelt down beside it…I think I said I was sorry a hundred times."[271] The reason this battle was destined to end in our favor in spite of the losses according to Lt. Col. Rainey was,

> *The difference is the enemy* doesn't have the young sergeants like we do and the fire team leaders…When you make contact, four enemy equals four fighters; for us, though, four Marines or four Soldiers equal a well-trained fire team led by competent leadership. Go where I go. Do what I do. That carried the day in every single engagement…[272]

Our losses gave us quite an unexpected perspective to the ordeal in

---

269 Ibid.
270 Twaddell, 2006, 135.
271 McAllester, "Band of Brothers," A05.
272 Rainey, 2006, 128-29.

Fallujah. Lt. Col. Rainey expressed it perfectly and probably much better than any of us could have managed.

You can say our battalion fought a tough fight and only lost two guys, but to me that is ludicrous. Others may say it was a big success, but whenever you lose an American fighting man in your command, it was not a success. We accomplished our objectives, we destroyed the enemy, and it was a big victory for the US, but it's never going to be a great thing based on guys like that making the ultimate sacrifice for their country.[273]

Spc. Velez (center with glasses) preparing for the battle that would take his life
Source: Photo courtesy of Mike Erwin

---

273 Ibid., 129.

10. END OF MISSION

Nothing fires the warrior's heart more with courage than to find himself and his comrades at the point of annihilation, at the brink of being routed and overrun, and then to dredge not merely from one's own bowels or guts but from one's own discipline and training the presence of mind not to panic, not to yield to the possession of despair, but instead to complete those homely acts of order which Dienekes had ever declared the supreme accomplishment of the warrior: to perform the commonplace under far-from-commonplace conditions… A mind which can maintain its lightness will not come undone in war.[274]

— Steven Pressfield, *Gates of Fire*

On or about 19 November, we were informed by Col. Shupp and the 1st Marine Division leadership that the situation in Fallujah was under enough control that our battalion and RCT-7 (a few days later) would be released back to our original areas of responsibility (AORs). Almost as quick as the whole situation in Fallujah unfolded and fell in our laps, it was over. In the span of just about three weeks, we had moved hundreds of miles, were accepted into the Marine brotherhood, helped defeat a savage enemy in high intensity urban combat, lost two of our own, and were headed back to resume a vast and explosive AOR that still required a lot of work.

After all those events transpired in such a short time, how were we supposed to feel? The battalion had executed a similar drop in, drop out

---

274 Pressfield, 259, 130.

fight with the Marines in Najaf. Were we supposed to deal with every-thing that just happened the same as before? I will never claim to have seen or experienced the worst of the war in Iraq. I know that many, many others went through more than I ever did, but even I think those questions are hard to answer. Sometimes the best answer might just be, "I don't know yet." Writing this book has been one of the ways I have personally tried to comprehend my involvement in the Iraq War (all tours) and attempt to make sense of it all. I can only imagine what those who experienced more traumatic circumstances feel like on a daily basis. What did this conflict mean, how did it affect others and myself? Is the mission really over? Lt Gen. Moore believed,

> *There is no such thing* as closure for soldiers who have survived a war. They have an obligation, a sacred duty, to remember those who fell in battle beside them all their days and to bear witness to the insanity that is war.[275]

For me personally, I have my other "ghosts" that I deal with just like all combat veterans. I ask myself everyday was the price worth it? I'd like to think so. I was extremely fortunate to escape Iraq with no close calls (that I know of), which has left me after the fact still waiting for my come to Jesus moment. Every day is a patrol. Everywhere I go some-one (the enemy) is out to get my family or me. How else could I have managed to go unscathed? I feel guilty. I know so many that sacrificed much more than I did… be it life, limb, or other wounds. To see those you know or care about sacrifice so much, and you make it through un-harmed, leaves you feeling guilty…there is nothing more you can really say about it. I do not think that feeling will ever go away either.

I am sure of a few things, however, and one of those is I love and respect Marines just as much as any Soldier, and I believe after Fal-

---

275 Lt. Gen. Hal Moore and Joseph L. Galloway, *We Are Soldiers Still: A Journey Back to the Battlefields of Vietnam* (New York, NY: Harper Perennial, 2009), 155.

lujah the feeling was mutual. A small gesture that spoke a lot to how our Marine brethren viewed us was that Maj. Gen. Natonski requested and was approved to fly in 800,000 beers to celebrate the Marine Corps birthday, which was 10 November.[276] Everyone, of course, was fighting in the city at that time, but as we pulled out and fell in on our tent city after the battle at Camp Fallujah there were two beers for each of us to celebrate their birthday. If you did not know this, Marines do not invite just anybody to participate in their very sacred and hallowed traditions of The Corps.

(From left to right) Capts. Chapman, Tyler, Gray, and Conley
drinking Budweiser, courtesy of the Marines
Source: Photo courtesy of Mike Erwin

---

276 Natonski, 2007, 8.

Two important pieces of my daily uniform
Source: Photo courtesy of Coley Tyler.

Maj. Gen. Natonski also requested and was approved by the Marine Corp to allow the Army units in Fallujah to wear the 1MARDIV patch as their combat patch and they awarded us (2-7 CAV) the Navy Unit Commendation (NUC). I wear both my patch and NUC on my uniforms with extreme pride. Combat patches and unit citations are a very special and important piece of your uniform. Marines do not wear patches on their uniforms and there are not very many Army units authorized to wear the 1MARDIV combat patch. When you see one, you know where that person was and what they were doing to earn it. Naval unit awards are also distinct from Army unit awards (no gold frame around the award) and makes them easily noticed as well. The distinguished additions to the uniform are nice, but what is truly special is to know that our unit had such an important and lasting impact on the Marines that they chose to include us in their history. That is priceless.

Col. Shupp also demonstrated the appreciation he felt as a commander and the level of closeness that our battalion and his RCT shared with one another when he spoke about our efforts in Fallujah.

They're all my sons, and 2-7 was incredible. No one can ever take that away from them. We could not have had that success if it wasn't for that Army battalion...I think they felt the same way, that they could have never cleared those buildings unless they had Marine infantry with them to go in and do it... So at night, when those tankers shut down and knew there was Marine infantry around, they felt like a million bucks. I don't think you could have made a better team.[277]

He did not stop there either.

These guys are fighters. These are the best Soldiers I've ever seen in my life, and I'll tell you it was just an honor to have them with us...Those guys were part of Inchon...2-7 went into the meat grinder and they cleared the enemy off those streets and prepped the battle for the infantry. If those Army tankers were not there, we would have had many Marines killed in action. But together, as a team, they were probably able to give one of the most decisive urban victories I think our nation has ever seen, against an enemy that was determined to fight until the bitter end.[278]

And as always, Col. Shupp's actions spoke volumes and louder than words as displayed by his attendance at the battalion awards ceremony

277 Shupp, 2006, 64-65.
278 Ibid., 60, 65, 66-67.

just before he rotated out to see our Soldiers decorated for their herculean efforts in the face of the enemy, fighting for those who couldn't fight for themselves.

On 14 November 2005, Maj. Karcher received an email from both the Commander and S3 (Buhl and Griffin) of 3-1 Marines that simply said, "Remember where we were a year ago? Thanks."[279] We appreciated the Marine efforts in return as well. The fact was the Marines did the majority of the clearing and our job was to make the clearing easier. Maj. Karcher, in reference to the horrible business of clearing, put it best when he said, "I really hated watching them do that. That was one of the most painful events of my life, watching those brave guys go in there and do that."[280] Words cannot express the awe and wonder at those boys who were doing that on a daily basis, day in and day out for weeks. Lt. Col. Rainey echoed the comments of both Col. Shupp and Maj. Karcher asserting,

> *I was struck and amazed* and will forever be humbled by the selflessness and lethality of the American fighting man: Marine and Soldier, tanker and infantryman. They are an unbelievable treasure that our country has. It's not about leading them in combat; it's about watching them and serving with them. To watch these guys look at a building full of bad guys that they know are in there, to watch them look at their buddy and look at their team leader and go, "Hell yea, we can do this." They went building after building, block by block and won every single fight. This is Fallujah, the last stronghold, the last bastion of the insurgency, the most diehard guys — and these young fire teams, these squads and platoons just whipped their ass.[281]

I do not think our feelings could be expressed any better than that.

---

279 Karcher, 2006, 206.
280 Ibid., 207.
281 Rainey, 2006, 132.

Command Sgt. Maj. Mace who was always very direct, simply stated when referring to the teamwork exhibited in Fallujah, "The rivalry crap between Marines, the Air Force, Navy—that stuff doesn't survive the first bullet."[282] I whole-heartedly agree.

So, what does it all mean? I was once asked about how many insurgents we had killed in Fallujah and I responded, "Honestly, I don't think too many people were concentrating on a body count. If it was clear that the Marines were able to do what they needed to do because we did our jobs, that was good enough for us."[283] MAJ Karcher more adeptly and eloquently expressed my feelings stating,

> *There's never glory when you're* killing people or when your soldiers are dying. That's not one of those things that, once you've done, that you really relish. I'm very proud of having been there. I'm very proud of the contribution that our unit made. I thought we did some great work and I thought we probably saved a bunch of American lives in the process. But it's still killing, and if you can ever put a pretty face on that, then you're a better (or worse) man than I am.[284]

Lt. Gen. Moore would reinforce with, "There is no glory in war—only good men dying terrible deaths…hate war, love the American warrior."[285]

---

282 Mace, 2006, 190.
283 Coley D. Tyler, interview by Matt Matthews, April 20, 2006, 145.
284 Karcher, 2006, 209.
285 Moore and Galloway, 121; Kingseed, 25.

PART III

EPILOGUE

EPILOGUE

ECHOES

A king does not abide within his tent while his men bleed and die upon the field. A king does not dine while his men go hungry, nor sleep when they stand at watch upon the wall. A king does not command his men's loyalty through fear nor purchase it with gold; he earns their love by the sweat of his own back and the pains he endures for their sake. That which comprises the harshest burden, a king lifts first and sets down last. A king does not require service of those he leads but provides it to them. He serves them, not they him.[286]

—Steven Pressfield, *Gates of Fire*

Leadership in the Army is by far the single most important aspect in determining significance for a unit. I purposefully avoid using the term success because significance in my mind implies an intangible and superior level of accomplishment. Significance has a deeper meaning that stands the test of time, unlike simple success; a term invariably considered fleeting and associated with purely winning, victory, triumph, etc. Lt. Gen. Moore cautioned leaders to "understand that what we may achieve is not who we are. There is a difference."[287]

Success is not what keeps soldiers coming back repeatedly to serve in

---

286 Pressfield, 360.
287 Moore, 66.

some of the worst conditions possible on earth. It is the indescribable feel-ings of such an intimate connection with those around you that you would do anything for them. Soldiers do not sacrifice themselves for glory and medals, but risk and often lose their lives out of love for their fellow brother. It is an impossible feeling to explain to those who have never been through the crucible of war. There is something about meeting a good death side-by-side with your brother in combat or losing your own life to save theirs in the pursuit of a noble cause that puts a warrior at peace and leaves them content. You know at that point you did it right and your brothers will say, "Well done, be thou at peace." In no way is it easy to handle or deal with, but your brothers are worth it. A spouse or civilian may never truly under-stand, but a good one will respect and embrace the uncommon valor that resides in the Soldier's core being and be thankful for it.

Great leaders foster these types of feelings in significant units. Units with great leaders will achieve success as a byproduct as they move on to an unequalled and transcendent level of group devotedness. One such leader with this ability to foster such esprit de corps through his words, actions, and way of life was retired Lt. Gen. Harold "Hal" Moore. Many 2-7 CAV leaders personified the essence of Lt. Gen. Moore and were a new generation of leaders, which would make him very proud. I hope he knows that I believe he realized his wish to never "be defined by others in terms of what was achieved, but rather who [was] Hal Moore, the man—[his] actions, decisions, comportment, [his] awareness of the shortness of life and the length of eternity."[288]

I am so thankful that back in my plebe year I made the choice to select Lt. Gen. Moore as my professional role model and served with so many in 2-7 CAV that reminded me of him. My self-assessment is I have come nowhere close to being as good a leader as Lt. Gen. Moore was, but he and my Ghost brothers continue to provide me an example to strive for in my quest to improve myself every day.

---

288 Ibid.

A mentor of mine at West Point, Col. Tony Burgess, helped me identify the type of leadership I see embodied by Lt. Gen. Moore and the Ghosts of Fallujah. This form of leadership has a more profound purpose than the accomplishments of the leader or success in the here and now. Generational Leadership is the idea that a leader makes such a significant impact that subordinates emulate them and begin to lead, teach, and mentor their own subordinates in the same way. This type of leader changes Soldiers' lives several generations removed and probably does not even know it. A generational leader's goal is to elevate those below them into a position so they achieve more than they ever did themselves.

Lt. Gen. Moore "always considered 'achievements of the led' to be a most important measuring tool [to judge what kind of leader you were]. It never was about rank with me. Wherever I was, I wanted my troopers to achieve their full potential." [289] Lt. Gen. Moore was this type of leader; the type of leader I attempt to be. When someone asks me where did I learn that or why do I do things the way I do, I can say, "Do you know about Lieutenant General Hal Moore? Have you heard of the Ghosts of Fallujah?" This type of leadership is spreading "mustard seeds" in a similar fashion as described in *Matthew 13: 31-32*. The mustard seed is the smallest of seeds, seemingly insignificant, but grows into the largest of garden plants, becoming a tree that provides for other living creatures. Lt. Gen. Moore's theory is

> ... *[l]eaders should be planting* mustard seeds. Most seeds will die. The few that see the light of day should be examined. The very few that strongly and forcefully rear their heads in the most unlikely of places, without cultivation and nourishment, could very well be the next world power, great corporation, or leader of his or her time. [290]

---

289 Ibid., 3.
290 Ibid., 49.

In the next few pages, I share some of the leadership lessons I learned from Lt. Gen. Moore and the Ghosts of Fallujah. They contain the most meaningful and consequential pieces of advice I learned from these great human beings and that I have tried to incorporate into my own personal leadership style. To begin with, leadership is not something you hide away and covet as a personal treasure and it is not a contest to see who can do it the best. That attitude goes against everything leadership is supposed to be, because "[l]eadership was never meant to be the 'survival of the fittest and the few, but for the finest and the all.'"[291]

HEART AND SOUL

Too many leaders in today's Army believe they have to lead without showing compassion, love, mercy, and tenderness. Not to be cliché, but I truly believe that fear, hate, enmity, and indignation are the emotions that lead to the real-world "dark side." A tender warrior leads from the heart and soul. Lt. Gen. Moore suggests that

> ... *[i]f more of us* led others by our soul rather than backbone, we might be better equipped to deal with our world and humanitarian issues. When the backbone leads, the soul may be left behind. When the soul leads, the only way it can lead is through the backbone. Soul first. Backbone second and supportive.[292]

Many selected leaders can learn the textbook methods of leadership, but ultimately fail in implementation because they lack the emotional will required to authentically inspire others to action. In other words, "Leadership is best when it begins in the heart and is not necessarily

---

291 Moore, "Memorial Day Letter to America's Youth," http://americanprofile.com/articles/memorial-day-letter-to-americas-youth/.
292 Moore, "No Holds Barred: A Leadership Conversation with LTG Hal Moore", 7.

something learned in a book from an old soldier."[293] In Lt. Gen. Moore's experience,

When training others to lead, I have found that the "how-to" lead can be taught. What cannot be taught is the "heart-to" lead. One can learn every aspect of every task, but if the heart to lead is lacking, one can only get by with the "how-to" for so long and then it will catch up to them.[294]

Leading from the heart and soul is not a 9-to-5 job. It is a full-time affair and does not just include subordinates. A subordinate's performance is often a reflection of their home life. A leader is not only responsible for their direct subordinates, but also their family. Families remain when uniformed service is over and they are worth the long-term investment. According to Lt. Gen. Moore, "Families are the secret strength of those working long and hard hours, year after year. The more respect given to one's family [yours and others], the greater the odds of the leaders reaching their potential."[295]

In Fallujah, one of my Soldier's closest relatives (his grandfather) passed away. This man basically raised this young Soldier, but due to the circumstances of the battle there was no way I could send him home to be at the funeral. He was mad, angry, sad, and hurting inside. He also realized the magnitude of the mission that faced us and accepted my offer to talk, smoke, and just sit with him for company. Imagine two grown men, one in pain, one there commiserating with a brother, beneath the fireworks of a raging battle. I would like to think that was leading with the heart.

As a company commander, I made it a point while we were deployed to send a monthly newsletter back to the Family Readiness Group. It

---

293 Ibid., 35.
294 Ibid., 32.
295 Ibid., 61.

was a small gesture that I think went a long way to keeping the families connected to what we were doing and experiencing. I learned this from Maj. Scott Jackson, my XO in 2-7 CAV. In the end, Lt. Gen. Moore learned that, "the most successful method of helping others to be without equal [was]—encouragement… encouragement is oxygen for the soul—and is forever remembered."[296] Families included.

FOLLOW ME!

Always lead from the front, lead by example, and personify the infantry motto of "Follow me!" This is a cornerstone of basic leadership. This is one of the primary expectations of any leader at any level. In Lt. Gen. Moore's mind, "To lead, one has to lead. Be the first into a situation and be the last one out."[297] Lt. Col. Rainey mentioned this on many occasions in Fallujah. It was one of the characteristics that set us apart from the enemy and ensured the outcome of the battle. A good leader never puts their subordinates into a situation they are not willing to lead them into and stay with them until the very end. The leader's life is no more special than the lowliest private's is and leader and follower are meant to share the dangers together. The leader should have nothing to fear about what will happen to the unit if they die, as long as they have done their job, which is prepare men to take your place.[298] A leader must be seen, cannot hide, and must walk the line because

> … [s]uccessful leaders know when to show up. Successful leaders know when to stand up. Successful leaders know when to speak up. The most important of the three is often showing up and the

---

296 Ibid., 80.
297 Ibid., 25.
298 Kingseed, 24.

next two follow only if appropriate. Leaders should not get these out of order.[299]

A leader does not always have to be the center of attention, but they must be present in the thick of the action. Subordinates will always notice a leader's absence and it will have severe negative ramifications throughout the force. Not sharing in the hardships, the same as the rest, is one of the quickest ways to lose the respect and trust of your subordinates. Lt. Gen. Moore's address to 1-7 CAV as they left for Vietnam in 1965 personifies these ideas perfectly.

We're moving into the valley of the shadow of death, where you will watch the back of the man next to you, as he will watch yours… I can't promise you that I will bring you all home alive, but this I swear: When we go into battle, I will be the first one to set foot on the field, and I will be the last to step off. And I will leave no one behind.[300]

As a company commander, I made it a point to patrol with my platoons on a regular basis, even if I was not the patrol leader, just to share in the hardships they were experiencing. I personally led all company-level missions and accepted no special treatment. I did not deploy my company to Iraq in 2006, but I was in command when we left fourteen months later and made sure I was on the last flight home. These were simple actions and gestures on my part that I would hope are still meaningful to my former Soldiers. I witnessed the same behavior in Fallujah with every level of leader in the battalion — Follow Me!

---

299 Moore, "No Holds Barred: A Leadership Conversation with LTG Hal Moore", 9, 39.
300 Moore, "Memorial Day Letter to America's Youth".

RLTW

When placed in a leadership position, it is very important to set the tone early with respect to expectations. This applies not only to the leader's expectations of their subordinates, but to also what the subordinates should expect of the leader. Doing this lays the foundation for two-way accountability. Simply expressed by Lt . Gen. Moore as, "I will do my best. I expect the same from each of you."[301] My expectations have always been grounded in the *Ranger Creed*. Graduating from Ranger School and earning my Tab is one the proudest moments of my life. The values imbued upon my character and the lessons I learned about myself will be with me for the rest of my life — a part of who I am. That is what I demand of myself and the standard I ask others to expect of me.

THE RANGER CREED [302]

Recognizing that I volunteered as a Ranger, fully knowing the hazards of my chosen profession, I will always endeavor to uphold the prestige, honor, and high espirit de corps of the Rangers.

Acknowledging the fact that a Ranger is a more elite Soldier who arrives at the cutting edge of battle by land, sea, or air, I accept the fact that as a Ranger my country expects me to move further, faster, and fight harder than any other soldier.

Never shall I fail my comrades. I will always keep myself mentally alert, physically strong and morally straight and I will shoulder more than my share of the task whatever it may be, one-hundred-percent and then some.

---

301 Lt. Gen. Hal Moore and Joseph L. Galloway, *We Were Soldiers Once...And Young* (Shrewsbury, UK: Airlife Publishing Ltd., 1994), 18.

302 Neal R. Gentry, "The Ranger Creed," US Department of the Army, http://www.army.mil/values/ranger.html.

Gallantly will I show the world that I am specially selected and well-trained Soldier. My courtesy to superior officers, neatness of dress and care of equipment shall set the example for others to follow.

Energetically will I meet enemies of my country. I shall defeat them on the field of battle for I am better trained and will fight with all my might. Surrender is not a Ranger word. I will never leave a fallen comrade to fall into the hands of the enemy and under no circumstances will I ever embarrass my country.

Readily will I display the intestinal fortitude required to fight on to the Ranger objective and complete the mission though I be the lone survivor.

Rangers Lead The Way!

In the military, life and death boils down to training, discipline, and trust in your unit and brothers to the left and right; the ability to execute at such a high level that the enemy is incapable of resistance. To accomplish this the leader has to develop "stressful realistic training, rigorous physical conditioning, and 'stern, fair and square discipline.'"[303] In the Department of Physical Education at West Point, our motto was "Set the Standard, Maintain the Standard." Creeds, mottos, or mantras are a good way to build trust and discipline, because "[o]nly by instilling layer after layer after layer of personal discipline on one's troops will units stand tall, hang in, and stay alive when the going gets tough."[304] In 2-7 CAV, *Gates of Fire* reflected the expectations of our leadership. Extremely high expectations, but not surprising considering the type of individuals that comprised our battalion.

---

303 Kingseed, 24.
304 Ibid.

KEEP ON THE SUNNY SIDE

A leader "can either contaminate his environment and his unit with his attitude and actions, or inspire confidence."[305] I always remind myself and others to stay on the sunny side. There are some bad days in the military, but they are even worse if you cannot find the silver lining or some positive aspect. My fire support team was deployed to Kuwait immediately following 9/11 as part of the buildup for Operation Enduring Freedom. My second commanding general in 1CD, Maj. Gen. Joe Peterson, came to visit around Christmas time (2001) and he told us a quick story that puts this in perspective. He told us about two children, as part of a study, put in separate rooms full of horseshit. One child was distraught, crying, and considered their predicament to be the worst possible situation because there were no toys. The other, to the researchers' surprise, was hooting and hollering, throwing shit everywhere, and digging around. The researchers asked the child what he was doing and he responded, "In all this shit, there has to be a pony somewhere!" Find the pony.

Negativity or a bad attitude is a roadblock to achieving significance and having the ability to encourage your subordinates to be without equal. The road of life is bumpy and it has many difficulties. As a leader, you have to display a sense of purpose and behavior that subordinates want to follow. Subordinates want to follow a positive leader and someone who can help them navigate all life throws at them. You have to have the right outlook and "[y]ou've got to have a dream in this life to move towards or you're dead in the water. And, once you realize that dream, accomplish that goal—get another!"[306] Remember it takes more work to frown than it does to smile!

---

305 Ibid.
306 Moore, "No Holds Barred: A Leadership Conversation with LTG Hal Moore", 31.

LIFE ISN'T FAIR

There is a saying in the Army that if events can go wrong, they will. We call this phenomenon "Murphy's Law" and you always do your best to prepare for the inevitable catastrophe. The enemy and random unforeseen events that are out of your control have a vote in how things unfold. The leader is charged with building resilience in themselves and the unit to deal with such setbacks. Lt. Gen. Moore would say to face up to the facts, deal with them, and move on to the next situation because the truth is… the best leaders with the most positive attitudes "live every day flexible and ready for change…For great leaders, change is expected and seized as moments of opportunity."[307]

The hard part is realizing and being comfortable in the fact that the changes may not actually be in your favor, but they are an opportunity nonetheless. Sometimes outside events are not what are making accomplishment of the mission difficult. On many occasions, you may be in a quandary because of your own failure. No one is perfect and people fail. The greatest fail often and learn from their mistakes, always improving and getting better at what they do. The best of the best "know how to adjust, how to learn, and how to deal with failure."[308] The only true failure is quitting and giving up.

PEOPLE IN GLASS HOUSES…

Most people have heard the saying, "people in glass houses don't throw stones." This adage holds true for leaders, too. A leader cannot be hypocritical and expect a certain level of character and discipline in the actions of their subordinates if they cannot do it themselves. Before someone can become a leader of others, they must realize "[t]he first person

---

307 Ibid., 14, 20.
308 Ibid., 33.

you must learn to lead is yourself."[309] The best way to learn this is by being at the bottom of the totem pole. There is a reason West Point brings in the best of the best out of high school and immediately subjects them to an environment where they are vulnerable, exposed, under pressure, and have no status. Beast Barracks teaches a new cadet how to follow and follow well. This is how grooming leaders begins because "[l]eaders learn, and learn, and learn. One has to know how to follow another before he or she can lead others."[310]

Once a leader, you should always remember to be sympathetic to the situation of your subordinates, because you have been there. A few things a good leader would be wise to remember, based upon this experience, is the "tongue can be a very dangerous weapon," which most of us use too frequently and without enough thought. Uncontrolled wrath or loss of temper by a leader makes them useless and damages subordinates, sometimes permanently.[311] A leader must always keep their wits about them and the ability to make a decision, no matter how they feel emotionally. A leader can "[n]ever over-react..." and can "[n]ever, never overreact to an overreaction."[312] Combat is emotional, but the leader has to be the calm in the storm. The leader must be the force in the unit that can steady the group and channel their emotional energy towards the accomplishment of the mission. The leader must be the standard-bearer of discipline and demeanor, both emotionally and physically. Lt. Col. Rainey understood this as he expressed his role in combat.

I work very hard every day to make sure I am using the right language, tone, and delivery when I speak with those around me. I have a temper that has gotten the best of me on several occasions in my life. Nothing good came of my outbursts and it took more work to repair the damage in the end than if I had just exercised better self-discipline

---

309 Ibid., 34.
310 Ibid., 10.
311 Ibid., 19, 76.
312 Ibid., 53.

to begin with. One of those instances was during company command (while deployed to Iraq) when I became agitated over a mandatory command program inspection (of our paperwork). In the middle of running combat missions, a high quality non-commissioned officer (who I had known for a very long time) wanted to give me a hard time (maintain the standard) over paperwork. Well, I unleashed my deadly tongue on him (who was not at fault for holding me to the Army mandated standards) and severely damaged my relationship with him. I learned from that lesson and am glad to say have not had a repeat occurrence. Never once in Fallujah did I experience a negative exchange. We needed all the positive energy we could muster and our leaders provided it.

DON'T FEAR THE REAPER

The stakes are high in combat. They are very high; they are a matter of life and death. Those under your command and those you care about will die even if you do everything right; they will die when you mess up; and they will die due to events out of your control because the enemy gets a vote. A leader must remain objective and in control, even when their troops are dying around them. They have an obligation to those still alive to do everything in their power to see them through to safety. A good Soldier and leader is never unafraid. Instead, they face that fear, use it to their benefit, and fight on to the objective regardless. Lt. Gen. Moore befittingly put fear in a Soldier's perspective.

> *But with respect to fear,* I have personally always faced it head on. There is a joy in facing fear that is difficult to express. One becomes hyper aware of everything around you. Time seems to be in slow motion. No sense of fear or panic. Intense focus on the task at hand. You feel unhurried. Your brain expands. Senses open up. The higher brain is at full speed. I recall learning somewhere

about the "mother of safety"—where one's mind and body adapt knowing the difference between life-enhancing excitement and primitive demise. Remember—-fear quivers; fear says "later;" fear is defeat; fear tears us down; fear is a thief; fear retreats. There is little about fear that I believe works in leadership. Emerson said, "Do the things you are afraid to do." You will grow stronger. Face up to your fears. We all have them. [313]

It takes a lot of guts to do this and not everyone is cut out for it. My definition of courage is facing your worst fears and executing the mission anyway to accomplish what needs to be done because it is the right thing to do. The implications will stay with you the rest of your life too because "[w]hen your men die and you don't, you feel guilty. That's all I can say about that."[314] Survivor's guilt is an extremely strong emotion that is very difficult to deal with on a daily basis. Many focus on bettering their lives to make the sacrifice of others worthwhile (picture the cemetery scene of *Saving Private Ryan*). Often they are quiet, unassuming and "if [they] handle [their] life with humility, it is because [their] life has been paid for by the blood, the cripplings, and the deaths of those who served under and with [them] on the battlefields."[315]

I personally suffer from this and ask myself every day why I made it when so many others did not, so many others that were far better human beings than I am. I think many old Soldiers find solace and strength in their faith. I rely heavily on mine, but also found an outlet in tattoos. My tattoos are constant reminders of what is important in my life and encouragement when I am feeling down and out. They are a visual expression of everything that weighs on my chest, on my heart, and on my mind. The truth is… death will eventually come for us all and we are all,

---

313 Ibid., 36.
314 Kingseed, 25.
315 Moore, "No Holds Barred: A Leadership Conversation with LTG Hal Moore", 52.

in fact, dead men walking. It is best to come to grips with that sooner rather than later.

HUMBLE PIE

The best diet for a leader includes many generous portions of humble pie. The leader's needs or wants are never above what is best for the unit. What the unit accomplishes is never the sole doing of the leader. Lt. Gen. Moore would tell you "[s]acrifice is the name of the game" because "I know the truth about who wins battles; the troops down in the ranks."[316] It is not enough to just know this important fact either. A leader must express and acknowledge their appreciation by "recognizing, giving credit, promoting, and rewarding!"[317] Col. Shupp and Lt. Col. Rainey's actions before, during, and after Fallujah illustrated this point precisely.

A leader who understands where success of the unit comes from will more effectively empower (develop) their subordinates, too. Lt. Gen. Moore warned us that,

> *The more a leader needs* to control, the less effective he or she becomes…When in fact, the more a leader gives up control by powering down, the more effective they become as leaders. Giving up control is a very mature leadership action and serves well when leading others.[318]

A set of great examples were the flexibility given to Capt. Twaddell by Lt. Col. Rainey and Maj. Jackson to fight as he saw fit (seizing of OBJs Kentucky and Ohio and in the Martyrs). A leader who has not

---

316 Ibid., 1, 18.
317 Ibid., 48.
318 Ibid., 17.

learned to truly enjoy humble pie will never be able to give up control the way it needs to be to ensure significance. One of the proudest moments of my company command had nothing to do with me; I was just happy I got to participate in the ceremony. One of my Soldiers, a cook, nicknamed "Steak," earned the Bronze Star with Valor device for a fierce engagement in downtown Baqubah, Iraq in 2007.

With his .50 caliber machine gun, he single-handedly, under intense fire from the enemy, suppressed and held at bay several dozen enemy insurgents so his platoon could withdraw from a local bank, from which they were escorting the Provincial Reconstruction Team to and from. There was only one-way out, they were surrounded, and Steak provided just enough time to allow them to get out before they were trapped. Presenting Steak that medal was the highlight of my command. My only hope is the vision we had set for our company in some way assisted him achieving that level of distinguished action in combat on behalf of his team.

JEDI KNIGHT

I have always heard from seasoned military leaders that the most important six inches on the battlefield is the six inches between a leader's ears. What goes on in the leader's mind will make or break a battle and decide victory or defeat. Do not get me wrong and think that physical fitness is not important. On the contrary, it is the elemental foundation for military leadership. Only after you have mastered the physical demands of combat can you then truly focus on development of the mind. This was the primary reason I chose to become a physical education instructor at West Point; to instill high expectations and standards in future officers about physical fitness as it relates to combat and the warrior ethos.

Lt. Gen. Moore believed physical and mental fitness were inextricably linked, "The more I was fit, the better leader I was...Mental alertness and smart decision-making feeds off being physically fit."[319] One of the Army's most intellectually prestigious and challenging schools, the School of Advanced Military Studies (SAMS), demands high levels of physical fitness. SAMS graduates, "Jedi Knights", are expected to set the standard intellectually and physically; to be the best of the best. Lt. Col. Jim Rainey, Majs. Scott Jackson, and Tim Karcher were my first exposure to SAMS graduates. Three graduates all serving in the same battalion was a professional experience that set my expectations of officers extremely high. Their performance spoiled me is the bottom line. Their excellence spread itself throughout our battalion. They personified everything I just laid out with respect to leadership. It's no wonder 2-7 CAV Ghost was such a significant unit for me and for history. I never thought I would do well enough or be considered smart enough to attend SAMS myself, but somehow, someway I was selected to attend in 2014 (2nd order effect of that generational leadership, no doubt).

SAMS taught me to be comfortable with ambiguity (planning under conditions of uncertainty), to be more concerned with probabilities, and be distrustful of absolutes (clear cut victory is impossible, but continuing advantage over your enemies is possible).[320] A Jedi must understand the environment around them; must understand where the environment evolved from, and how to act within the environment to achieve desired outcomes. A Jedi has a genuine appreciation for Complex Systems Theory that will influence how they make decisions and convey information to others. A Jedi should be able to take their understanding of the complex environment around them and show their subordinates simplicity on the other side of complexity.

In Lt. Gen. Moore's words, "Vision sets the table, the objective, and

---

319 Ibid., 69.
320 Everett C. Dolman, *Pure Strategy: Power and Principle in the Space and Information Age*, ed. Colin Gray and Williamson Murray, Cass Series: Strategy and History (New York, NY: Frank Cass, 2005), 6; James N. Rosenau, "Thinking Theory Thoroughly," in *The Scientific Study of Foreign Policy*, ed. James N. Rosenau (London, UK: Frances Pinter, 1980), 34.

the end goal."[321] Through words, a Jedi must illuminate the path for the unit to achieve its mission. To do this, a Jedi must reflect on the past without focusing on it because what normal is for the mission in the present is unique.[322] In that frame of mind, the Jedi's plan should "concentrate on the probabilities and be prepared for the possibilities" of any given situation.[323] A Jedi is a contemplative leader, who generates positive action as a result. A Jedi is self-aware and knows, "[i]f there's a doubt in [their] mind, there's no doubt at all."[324] A Jedi is self-critical and is "always considering what [they are] NOT doing, what [they] should be doing, and what [they are] doing that they should NOT be doing."[325] A Jedi "draw[s] on their library of experience and evaluate[s] how they handled each problem" so they can apply lessons learned in the future.[326] The more those experiences grow and the more a Jedi draws upon those experiences, the faster the process becomes to the point of it being a gut feeling, intuition, or coup d'oeil ("stroke of the eye" or a comprehensive glimpse). Successful application of these instincts is the mark of the military genius. Fallujah required these traits on many occasions that only our three Jedis could have handled as well as they did.

THE DARK SIDE

The antithesis of the "light side" represented by leaders who are tender, humble, positive, and of high moral fiber is the "dark side." A leader beholden to this side is not driven by those characteristics we have discussed here that leave a legacy to emulate. These leaders fall prey to easy traps that can destroy them and/or their family (unit and personal alike).

---

321 Moore, "No Holds Barred: A Leadership Conversation with LTG Hal Moore", 8.
322 Ibid., 43, 57.
323 Ibid., 54.
324 Ibid., 51.
325 Ibid., 80.
326 Ibid., 29.

Lt. Gen. Moore believed a few of the easiest and most disastrous are 1) Letting success go to one's head; 2) Believing financial success [substitute military rank or honors or any other material possession] is the end all; 3) Thinking one's press clippings are true; and 4) Moving away from those relationships that helped you become successful."[327] You could characterize these leaders as "[r]eactive, lots of talk, scattered guidance, poor example, bad example and bad leadership in crisis—especially time—critical."[328] Every leader has both light and dark within them, the test and the struggle is which side you listen to, let guide your thoughts and actions, and define who you are.

I feel the grip and far off hold of those that have preceded me in the profession of arms and the weighty responsibility upon my shoulders to continue the great history of units in which I have served. I am touched and shepherded by the thoughts, ideas, and example of Lt. Gen. Moore and the Ghosts of Fallujah. Their wisdom and reflections are the echoes in my ears that continue to guide me in my military career and life endeavors.

I served personally with the Ghosts of Fallujah, but I was also very fortunate to meet Lt. Gen. Moore and his Command Sgt. Maj. from 1-7 CAV, Basil Plumley, during my time as an instructor at West Point in the spring of 2010. These chances to become a part of the history of the 7th Cavalry had a huge impact and meant a lot to me. I cannot adequately express in words the impression of Lt. Gen. Moore and the Ghosts of Fallujah have had on my life personally and militarily. I consider myself privileged to have served with such a significant unit and learned from so many of its members—past and present.

Over the years since the conclusion of the Second Battle of Fallujah, I have finally figured out that our combat mission may have been completed, but for all of us that were there so many years ago there is another mission still ongoing. A mission many veterans are on right now

327 Ibid., 21.
328 Ibid., 54.

and Paul Harvey would call the rest of the story. The mission is life. This is a life that after over a decade of conflict, numerous deployments, other battles, and other experiences that have changed the lives of service members and their families. Many of these changes are proving too hard or difficult for some to bear. The other ghosts of Fallujah remain.

They are the residual emotions, feelings, and sensations—apparitions (ghosts) if you will—that are haunting many, not just the Ghosts of Fallujah. It is important that we show we care and that we are here for one another. Veterans groups such as the Iraq and Afghanistan Veterans of America, US Army Ranger Association, 7th Cavalry Association, the 1st Cavalry Division Association and others offer an opportunity to get together and stay in touch with old friends. Other local chapters of National Veteran's organizations offer a helping hand and support veterans in need. Being a part of organizations that create a supportive network is very important. I try to keep in touch with many of my Toxin and Ghost brothers. The reason this is so important is that the legacy of many veterans is in jeopardy if we let the ghosts of combat take or ruin their lives.

To be able to function and contribute wherever you find yourself, you need to be able to take a hard, honest look at yourself and understand what is going on inside you—self-awareness. I mentioned in the very beginning that my invitation to Senior Night was the first time I forced myself to take a deep introspective look at my life. That introspection led me back to the influence of Lt. Gen. Moore and my time with the Ghosts of Fallujah. From that point on, my life changed and I was guided by some principles that are not new, but newly discovered, or understood, and taken to heart by me. This is what I shared with those graduating seniors that night in the suffocating heat of the Panther Den.

The first was an anonymous quote on a bumper sticker that hung in my daddy's office his entire career that read, "I asked God for all things that I might enjoy life; I was given life that I might enjoy all things." For years, I read those lines sitting up there in his office, but it never resonated with me on a deeper level. It took me facing the very real possibility of losing my life that I truly grasped the magnitude of what that person was trying to say. They were in fact just several lines of a full prayer credited to an unknown Civil War soldier.

"PRAYER OF AN UNKNOWN SOLDIER"[329]

I asked God for strength, that I might achieve;
    I was made weak, that I might learn humbly to obey.
I asked for health, that I might do greater things;
    I was given infirmity, that I might do better things.
I asked for riches, that I might be happy;
    I was given poverty, that I might be wise.
I asked for power, that I might have the praise of men;
    I was given weakness, that I might feel the need of God.
I asked for all things, that I might enjoy life;
    I was given life, that I might enjoy all things.
I got nothing that I asked for, but everything I hoped for.
    Almost despite myself, my unspoken prayers were answered.
I am among all men most richly blessed.

                                            —Anonymous

Life has so much to offer, but you have to be willing to open up to all of it to enjoy your life in all its glory. That prayer also made me realize that life is too short and you must live in the moment.

It is such a travesty to wish time away to try to get to the completion of your next hurdle or goal so you can move on. Trust me, I know. It is the way I was wired growing up and I have spent countless time unwiring that part of my personality. If you spend your life trying to

329 Anonymous, "Prayer of an Unknown Soldier," WikiChristian, http://www.wikichristian.org/wiki/en/index.php?title=Prayer_Of_An_Unknown_Soldier.

accomplish goals just for accomplishment's sake, then you will realize it is empty. Time will pass you by as you are always concentrating on what is next. It may be cliché, but you have to stop and smell the roses every chance you get (which does not mean do not have goals — just do not let them run your life). My life has been so much richer since I have started to take pleasure in the smallest things. Some are simply the sounds of my children's laughter, the wonder of the universe in the night sky, the sound of Katydids in the summer swelter of Western North Carolina, hunting, and hiking. These things and many similar simple pleasures make me smile and feel content. They make a huge difference in a cruel world.

The last insight I shared was about the joke that the person with the most toys when they die wins. I told them in gentler terms that was a load of you know what. When you die, you will not win or lose an earthly contest. You will, however leave an earthly legacy, which is relationships. Your legacy will be people. Your legacy is going to be what people remember about you. These memories could be of a summer day spent swimming, eating ice cream, and joy riding in a Jeep in central Texas. It could be a contagious smile when you are hungry, tired, dirty, and just needing a bright moment when a patrol never seems to end. Maybe it is just a squeeze of your arm and a look in the eye of someone very close that says, "I love you more than you can imagine," not knowing that would be the last time you would see them alive.

This journey that I have been sharing with you, that started back in the Spring of 1997 (or earlier), came full circle in April 2010. The occasion was the visit of Lt. Gen. Moore with Command Sgt. Maj. Plumley to West Point for the unveiling of Lt. Gen. Moore's dedication panels in the Competitive Sports Hallway in the Arvin Cadet Physical Development Center at the United States Military Academy. That day was one of the most memorable days of my life and it was so much more important than 13 years prior because I had now become a part of and contributed to the legacy that both those men had already lived up to and were so instrumental in continuing in their time.

Author (left) meeting retired Lt. Gen. Moore (center) for the second time in 2010 at West Point with retired Command Sgt. Maj. Plumley (right)
Source: Photo courtesy of Coley Tyler

Throughout this journey, I have continued to evolve and have started to accumulate many experiences and lessons learned that I will use in the future. I know this journey I am on cannot be neatly concluded because it's not over, but because I am somewhat obsessive compulsive, I felt compelled to have something a little bit more tangible at this stage to help me capture some of the most important thoughts I have adopted as part of who I am.

Because of my mild case of obsessive compulsive disorder, which to some who know me may say is not really all that mild; I am a list guy. I have a list for everything to make sure I do not forget anything, driven by the horrible fear of forgetting some important detail or task and letting it slip through the cracks only to come bite me in my backside later on.

So, I have generated a list, go figure, for my life philosophy and foundation. Before we get to this list, it helps to understand that the foundation is based in a song and a mountain. Lt. Gen. Moore believed, "all of us need to view ourselves in a common way…I am—just the way I am—a plain vanilla kind of guy."[330] For me, I am just the way I am—a simple man. I have sung, "Simple Man" by Lynyrd Skynyrd to my children since the day they were born. It is the embodiment of who I am and I believe its words will serve them well one day. The mountain, Wayah Bald, has been my heaven on earth since I was little and looks over my town from the west, keeping me company constantly.

THE SIMPLE MAN'S GUIDE TO THE BALD LIFE

(Bald: Lacking a natural or usual covering; Lacking ornamentation; unadorned; Undisguised; blunt)

1. There is someone up above—love, follow, and have faith in God and his Son, Jesus Christ.

2. Live simply, don't live too fast—life is already too short, take time to enjoy it.

3. Troubles will come and they will pass—rise to those challenges and embrace them.

4. Find love, a soulmate—life is relationships, communication, connection, and legacy.

---

330 Moore, "No Holds Barred: A Leadership Conversation with LTG Hal Moore", 53.

5. Love and understand yourself—all that you need in life you can find in your soul, know where and what to look for.

6. Never, ever, stop learning and seeking knowledge.

7. You are never truly alone, you have never truly done anything on your own and that is okay—real joy comes from elevating the group or others above yourself.

8. Lead from the front or get out of the way—and when your followers have followed you as far as they can, be their first stepping stone, propelling them on their own journey as they surpass you—smile and be joyful in that occasion.

9. No matter what, never, ever give up, the only real failure is quitting; you can always be content with giving your best—a 110%.

10. Substance, not show—be humble .

11. Try and live every day like it was your last—because it could be and how you live does matter, it matters a lot.

GLOSSARY OF ACRONYMS

1CD: 1st Cavalry Division

A.D.: Anno Domini (In the year of our Lord)

A/S#: Assistant Officer

ALO: Air Liaison Officer

ALOC: Administrative and Logistical Operations Center

ANGLICO: Air Naval Gunfire Liaison Company

AO: Area of Operations

AOR: Area of Responsibility

AWOL: Absent Without Leave

B.C.: Before Christ

BAS: Battalion Aid Station

BDE: Brigade

BFV: Bradley Fighting Vehicle

BN: Battalion

CAS: Close Air Support

CASEVAC: Casualty Evacuation

CAV: Cavalry

CDO: Commando

CDR: Commander

CFL: Coordinated Fire Line

CO: Company

DIRLAUTH: Direct Liaison Authorized

FA: Field Artillery

FIST: Fire Support Team

FSC: Forward Support Company

FSE: Fire Support Element

FSO: Fire Support Officer

GBU: Guided Bomb Unit

HHC: Headquarters and Headquarters Company

IAF: Iraqi Armed Forces

ICM: Improved Conventional Munitions

IED: Improvised Explosive Device

IIF: Iraqi Intervention Force

IIG: Interim Iraqi Government

IN: Infantry

ING: Iraqi National Guard

IPB: Intelligence Preparation of the Battlefield

"ISR: Intelligence, Surveillance, and Reconnaissance"

JTAC: Joint Terminal Attack Controller

KIA: Killed in Action

LAR: Light Armored Reconnaissance

LD: Line of Departure

LOC: Line of Communication

LZ: Landing Zone

MARDIV: Marine Division

MEDEVAC: Medical Evacuation

MEF: Marine Expeditionary Force

MEU: Marine Expeditionary Unit

MNF-I: Multi-National Forces-Iraq

NCO: Non-Commissioned Officer

NUC: Navy Unit Citation

NVA: North Vietnamese Army

OBJ: Objective

OIF: Operation Iraqi Freedom

OPORD: Operations Order

PA: Physician's Assistant

PAVN: People's Army of Vietnam

PL: Phase Line

PL: Platoon Leader

PLT: Platoon

PSG: Platoon Sergeant

PUC: Presidential Unit Citation

RCT: Regimental Combat Team

ROE: Rules of Engagement

ROMAD: Radio Operator, Maintainer, Driver

ROTC: Reserve Officers' Training Corps

RPG: Rocket Propelled Grenade

S1: Personnel Officer

S2: Intelligence Officer

S3: Operations Officer

S4: Supply Officer

S5: Civil Affairs Officer

S6: Communications Officer

SAMS: School of Advanced Military Studies

SAW: Squad Automatic Weapon

"SEAL: Sea, Air, Land"

SSF: Specialized Special Forces (Iraqi)

TFSA: Task Force Supply Area

TIC: Troops in Contact

TOC: Tactical Operations Center

UAV: Unmanned Aerial Vehicle

US: United States

USAF: United States Air Force

USMA: United States Military Academy

USMC: United States Marine Corps

VBIED: Vehicle-borne Improved Explosive Device

BIBLIOGRAPHY

Anonymous. "Prayer of an Unknown Soldier." WikiChristian, http://www.wikichristian.org/wiki/en/index.php?title=Prayer_Of_An_Unknown_Soldier.

Army, US Department of the. "Army Regulation 600-8-22." Washington, D.C., 2015.

Association, Seventh United States Cavalry. "Seventh United States Cavalry Unit Decorations." http://us7thcavalry.com/7-cav-Reg-Decorations.htm.

———. "Seventh United States Cavalry Unit History." http://us7thcavalry.com/7-cav-regiment-historyIndex.htm.

Brooke, Chris. "Eyewitness to War: The US Army in Operation Al Fajr, an Oral History." By Matt Matthews (May 1, 2006): 263-79.

Camp, Richard D. *Battle for the City of the Dead: In the Shadow of the Golden Dome, Najaf, August 2004.* Minneapolis, MN: Zenith Press, 2011.

———. *Operation Phantom Fury: The Assault and Capture of Fallujah, Iraq.* Minneapolis, MN: Zenith Press, 2009.

Channel, The History. "First in Battle: The True Story of the 7th Cavalry." 2002.

Dolman, Everett C. *Pure Strategy: Power and Principle in the Space and Information Age.* Cass Series: Strategy and History. Edited by Colin Gray and Williamson Murray New York, NY: Frank Cass, 2005.

Erwin, Michael S. "Eyewitness to War: The US Army in Operations Al Fajr, an Oral History." By Matt Matthews (April 19, 2006): 47-56.

Gentile Jr., Lee. April 3, 2012.

Gentry, Keil R. "RCT-1 Fires in the Battle of Fallujah." *Field Artillery*, November-December 2005, 26-29.

Gentry, Neal R. "The Ranger Creed." US Department of the Army, http://www.army.mil/values/ranger.html.

Glass, Peter. "Eyewitness to War: The US Army in Operation Al Fajr, an Oral History." By Matt Matthews (March 29, 2006): 71-81.

Gott, Kendall D. *Eyewitness to War the US Army in Operation Al Fajr: An Oral History*. Edited by Jennifer Lindsey, Fort Leavenworth, Kansas, USA: Combat Studies Institute, 2009.

Huber, Thomas M. "The Battle of Manila." In *Block by Block: The Challenges of Urban Operations*, edited by William G. Robertson and Lawrence A. Yates, 91-122. Fort Leavenworth, KS: U.S. Army Command and General Staff College Press, 2003.

Hunt, Maj Todd M. "Operation Al Fajr: The Battle for Fallujah." 2004.

Jackson, Scott. "Linkedin Profile." LinkedIn.

Karcher, Tim. "Eyewitness to War: The US Army in Operation Al Fajr, an Oral History." By Matt Matthews (March 14, 2006): 199-209.

Kingseed, Cole C. "Beyond the Ia Drang Valley." *Army Magazine*, November 2002, 18-25.

Kolb, Richard K., Tim Dyhouse, and Janie Blankenship. "Heroes of Iraq." *VFW*, March 2012, 18-19.

Kolb, Richard K., and Kelly Von Lunen. "Iraq War Casualties." *VFW* 2012, 58-59.

Lamb, Robert, Jane Reilly, and Barbara Sanders, eds. *Bugle Notes '96* Vol. 88. West Point, NY, 1996.

Lawrence, Jim. April 2012.

Lowry, Richard S. *New Dawn: The Battles for Fallujah*. New York, NY: Savas Beatie LLC, 2010.

Mace, Timothy L. "Eyewitness to War: The US Army in Operation Al Fajr, an Oral History." By Matt Matthews (April 19, 2006): 185-94.

Mansur, Ahmed. *Inside Fallujah: The Unembedded Story*. Northampton, MA: Olive Branch Press, 2009.

Matthews, Matt M. *Operation Al Fajr: A Study in Army and Marine Corps Joint Operations*. Fort Leavenworth: Combat Studies Institute Press, 2006.

McAllester, Matthew. "Assault on Fallujah." *Newsday*, November 12, 2004, A07.

———. "Band of Brothers." *Newsday*, November 17, 2004, A05.

———. "Driving toward the heart of enemy." *Newsday*, November 9, 2004, A07.

———. "Grim reality, up close." *Newsday*, November 10, 2004, A02.

———. "Guerilla's Paradise." *Newsday*, November 14, 2004, A03.

———. "Linkedin Profile." LinkedIn.

———. "Long-planned attack begins." *Newsday*, November 8, 2004, A04.

———. "A lot of fighting to do still." *Newsday*, November 10, 2004, A02.

———. "Pockets of resistance." *Newsday*, November 15, 2004, A04.

———. "Urban War Strategy." *Newsday*, November 11, 2004, A03.

McGrath, John M. "Chapter 6: The Early Modern Brigade, 1958-1972." In *The Brigade: A History, Its Organization and Employment in the US Army*, 59-76. Fort Leavenworth, KS: Combat Studies Institute Press, 2004.

Moore, Lt. Gen. Hal. "Memorial Day Letter to America's Youth." http://americanprofile.com/articles/memorial-day-letter-to-americas-youth/.

———. "No Holds Barred: A Leadership Conversation with LTG Hal Moore." *DRAFT* (2009). Published electronically August 1, 2009. http://www.auburnschools.org/ahs/llalexander/HMLA/No%20 Holds%20Barred%20Hal%20Moore%20Conversation%20July%20 29%202009.doc.

Moore, Lt. Gen. Hal, and Joseph L. Galloway. *We Are Soldiers Still: A*

Journey Back to the Battlefields of Vietnam. New York, NY: Harper Perennial, 2009.

———. *We Were Soldiers Once...And Young.* Shrewsbury, UK: Airlife Publishing Ltd., 1994.

Morris, Sheldon. "Operational Leadership Experiences in the Global War on Terrorism." By Matt Matthews (April 23, 2006): 1-8.

Natonski, Richard F. "Operational Leadership Experiences in the Global War on Terrorism." By Laurence Lessard (April 5, 2007): 1-10.

Navy, US Department of the. "Navy Unit Commendation (NU)." https://awards.navy.mil/awards/webapp01.nsf/(vwAwardsDisp)/ AW-10052085MQQS?OpenDocument.

Pressfield, Steven. *Gates of Fire: An Epic Novel of the Battle of Thermopylae.* New York, NY: Bantam Dell, 1998.

Rainey, James. July 15, 2012.

———. "Eyewitness to War: The US Army in Operation Al Fajr, an Oral History." By Matt Matthews (April 19, 2006): 109-33.

Rosenau, James N. "Thinking Theory Thoroughly." In *The Scientific Study of Foreign Policy*, edited by James N. Rosenau, 19-31. London, UK: Frances Pinter, 1980.

Shupp, Michael. "Eyewitness to War: The US Army in Operation Al Fajr, an Oral History." By Matt Matthews (March 25, 2006): 47-69.

Smith, Jack P. "Sandbag for a Machine Gun: Jack P. Smith on the Battle of the Ia Drang Valley and the Legacy of the Vietnam War." http:// www.mishalov.com/death_ia_drang_valley.html.

Twaddell, Edward. "Eyewitness to War: The US Army in Operation Al Fajr, an Oral History." By Matt Matthews (February 28, 2006): 125-38.

Tyler, Coley D. "Eyewitness to War: The US Army in Operation Al Fajr, an Oral History." By Matt Matthews (April 20, 2006): 139-45.

Urrutia, John. "Eyewitness to War: The US Army in Operation Al Fajr, an Oral History." By Matt Matthews (March 14, 2006): 211-26.

Willbanks, James H. "The Battle of Hue, 1968." In *Block by Block: The*

Challenges of Urban Operations, edited by William G. Robertson and Lawrence A. Yates, 123-60. Fort Leavenworth, KS: US Army Command and General Staff College Press, 2003.

ABOUT THE AUTHOR

LTC Coley D. Tyler is an Active Duty US Army Officer and former member of the Second Battalion, Seventh Cavalry Regiment (2-7 CAV). He was the Battalion Fire Support Officer during the Second Battle of Fallujah. LTC Tyler has served in many capacities during his service as an Artillery Officer in the First Cavalry Division, Physical Education Instructor at the United States Military Academy, Space Operations Officer in Korea, and Space Integration Officer to the Maneuver Center of Excellence at Fort Benning, GA. He is married with four children.

CPSIA information can be obtained
at www.ICGtesting.com
Printed in the USA
FFHW01n0059131018
48756451-52835FF